SO-BLT-836

118286

PAUL AND THE EARLY CHRISTIANS

Carl F. Andry

UNIVERSITY
PRESS OF
AMERICA

Copyright © 1981 by

University Press of America, Inc.

P.O. Box 19101, Washington, D.C. 20036

All rights reserved

Printed in the United States of America

ISBN: 0-8191-1936-9 (Perfect)

ISBN: 0-8191-1935-0 (Cloth)

Except in some instances where the author has provided his own translations
of key words, phrases and sentences, the translation which is used throughout
this book is the Revised Standard Version of the Bible copyrighted 1946, 1952
© 1971, 1973, and is used by permission from the National Council of the
Churches of Christ in the U.S.A.

Library of Congress Catalog Card Number: 81-40766

5.924
81
2

L.I.F.E. College Library
1100 Glendale Blvd.
Los Angeles, Calif. 90026

Dedicated to the memory of a great teacher

HENRY JOEL CADBURY

032326

L.I.F.E. College Library
1100 Glendale Blvd.
Jeles, Calif. 90026

032326

ACKNOWLEDGEMENT

I am deeply gratified by the judgments of the late Dr. John R. Emens who was President of Ball State University; of Dr. Richard W. Burkhardt, formerly Vice President for Instructional Affairs and Dean of Faculties at Ball State University; and of Dr. James A. McClintock, M.D. who a few years ago awarded with the McClintock grant my efforts in this study of Paul. I am very grateful to Dr. McClintock who supplied this grant, which financial assistance has been a great source of encouragement in the preparation of this manuscript.

If this work generates in any readers an interest in the cause for which Paul labored, and serves to awaken an understanding in an unusual succession of events which occurred in the life of Paul and likewise in the life of the early Christians, it will prove worthy of the trust which Dr. Emens, Dr. Burkhardt and Dr. McClintock have placed in me, and I shall be more than content.

Carl F. Andry
Ball State University
Muncie, Indiana

god

will

survive

our

mistakes

CONTENTS

PREFACE

What are the major literary sources from which we can glean information about Paul the apostle? (1) Paul's letters and (2) The Acts of the Apostles.

How does western Christendom usually approach Paul? The general tendency is to approach him through The Acts of the Apostles, and there seems to be a preference for this approach. Why this preference? Paul is the central character of The Acts. It was designed to emulate his apostleship. Of all the books in the library of early Christianity now commonly referred to as the New Testament, The Acts of the Apostles is the one book which is popularly regarded as history. The attachment to history gives us the impression both consciously and unconsciously that The Acts is reliable, accurate and factual in everything which it says, whereupon the tendency in western Christendom is first of all to saturate the student with The Acts account of Paul. Where could we find a more excellent place to begin! And better still, The Acts of the Apostles is sanctified by inspiration, as are all the other books of the Bible, which makes it, since it is both history and inspired, doubly reliable, all of which means that as a source of information about Paul it cannot possibly lead us astray.

With these assumptions in both foreground and background we then proceed to structure Paul's life from The Acts report on him. We easily set our minds on an outline of his activities which revolves around three missionary journeys. This pattern, structuring Paul from The Acts, has become established so impregnably in our minds that to question the reliability of anything which the author of The Acts reports about Paul is a blatant defilement of the Sanctum Sanctorum. When we look subsequently into his letters our predispositions from The Acts of the Apostles are so firmly entrenched that we mould all information from his letters into The Acts pattern. And how is this process justified? It is a very legitimate process because Paul's letters are equally inspired, whereupon the information contained in his letters could fit no other way.

What is our foremost interest in this exploration of Paul and the early Christians? Our first and foremost interest is to quest for accurate information in the spirit of honesty. We want to establish a word picture of Paul which is as reliable and as accurate as we can possibly achieve. The traditional approach, structuring Paul from The Acts, then fitting all information from Paul's letters into The Acts pattern, has served only as a stumbling block to an appreciation of Paul and of his activities. What is its weakness? It gives primary significance to our secondary source; and, vice versa, it gives only secondary significance to our primary sources. What are these primary sources of information about Paul? None other than the letters which Paul himself wrote. They should come first. We should first structure

9

Paul's life from information which he gives about himself in his letters, and then we should treat The Acts information as subsequent.

When did Paul write his letters? 50-55 A.D. When did the author of The Acts of the Apostles write his emulation of Paul? Near 95 A.D., forty years after Paul disappeared from the scene probably martyred.

Whom are we to regard as having the more reliable information: (1) Paul himself as he relates his own experiences; or (2) an anonymous author who had no personal acquaintance with Paul? We presume it compatible with good judgment, certainly, as well as with good religious principles and with academic integrity, to regard the information which Paul gives about himself as more reliable.

The Christians of the western world have placed too much confidence in The Acts of the Apostles. Its author, who wrote approximately forty years after Paul disappeared from the scene, threw his book together haphazardly from a wide variety of unrelated sources. He was effected by traditions which had grown up about Paul, traditions which had been subjected to at least forty years of time erosion as well as to time build-up. But the traditions were spotty, and in his desire to fill in the missing parts which tradition had overlooked he took the liberty to invent the most unusual and fantastic things about Paul. He refashioned Paul to fit the preferences of a dogmatic and victorious gentile church, made Paul a hero of that church, then deliberately treated his 95 A.D. refashioned Paul as if he were the 29-55 A.D. apostle. This author mythicized Paul.

We are not superstitious about Paul's letters, about The Acts of the Apostles, or about any other literature either in or out of the Bible. And the fact of the matter is, the information which Paul gives about himself is the most reliable information about him which we have. Paul's letters, his reports about his own activities, are certainly and indisputably our primary sources for information about Paul. The information which Paul gives about himself in his letters usually comes through sporadically, unsystematically, unpredictably and unpremeditatedly. Such spontaneous expression is a better criterion for determining reliability than is the attachment of an enigma unwisely accepted as history, or than is sanctification by the attachement of a religious dogma in the form of inspiration, or than is the attempt to perpetrate any kind of a dogmatic point of view.

My accumulation of years has failed to enhance my appreciation for dogmatic and polemical dispositions.

Our foremost interest is to understand the 29-55 A.D. Paul from Paul's own reports about himself. To do this we must purge ourselves of conventional predispositions, reverse the tendency of western Christendom, proceed to structure Paul's life according to his reports about himself as we can understand him in his letters, give priority to primary sources, regard The Acts account as subsidiary, and examine Paul's reports about himself and the traditions and other reports about Paul recorded in The Acts of the Apostles the same as we would examine information contained in any other literature, then evaluate their relative merits. We will listen to the voice of Paul through his letters, that is, understand Paul according to Paul. We judge this to be the best way to gather up reasonable impressions of his activities. Even though the scope of this study goes somewhat beyond this nucleus, this interest, understanding Paul according to Paul, will remain central throughout.

PART I

INTRODUCTION

INTRODUCTION

Did Paul write down an account of his daily activities and preserve them in the form of a diary? We have no reason to judge that he did, and if he did no such diary has survived.

Did Paul, near the end of his life, reflect back to his earlier days and write an account of his reflections in the form of an autobiography? Again we have no reason to judge that he did, and if he did no such account of his life has prevailed.

Did Paul write anything about himself, his attitudes and activities? We are fortunate that he did. As a matter of fact the very earliest information which we are able to acquire about Paul comes to us 50-55 A.D. in documents from his own pen, or which he dictated to his secretary Tertius, documents in the form of letters. Some of these letters he wrote to churches which he founded: Philippi, Thessalonica, Corinth, Galatia. Others he wrote to churches which he did not found: Colossae, Laodicea, Ephesus (Paul might have established his own church in Ephesus), Rome. One letter he wrote to a personal friend and convert: Philemon.

Did any personal acquaintance of Paul, one who was a companion and eyewitness, take it upon himself to write an account of Paul's activities? No biography of Paul has survived, but some will insist that Luke worked with Paul and that he wrote an eyewitness account of Paul's activities in The Acts of the Apostles. This disposition raises two questions: (1) Was Luke a companion of Paul in his mission throughout Macedonia, Achaia and Asia Minor, that is, when Paul went into Philippi, Thessalonica, Corinth, Galatia or any other town or province to preach the gospel was Luke by his side? (2) Did Luke write The Acts of the Apostles?

If Luke traveled with Paul and worked with Paul he would have spent approximately two years with Paul in Philippi, two years with Paul in Thessalonica, one and one-half years with Paul in Corinth, one year or less with Paul in Galatia and approximately three years with Paul in Ephesus. Luke would have been acquainted personally with Paul's converts in these places. All would have been anxious to hear about Luke and to receive Luke's greetings through Paul when Paul wrote to them, and Paul would have been pleased certainly to send Luke's greetings to them. Paul sent greetings to the Philippians, the Thessalonians and the Corinthians from Timothy (Phil. 1:1, I Thes. 1:1, II Cor. 1:1). He sent greetings to the Thessalonians from Silas (I Thes. 1:1). He mentioned Timothy to the Philippians, the Thessalonians and the Corinthians in other respects (Phil. 2:19, I Thes. 3:2, 6, II Cor. 1:19). He mentioned Titus to the Corinthians and the Galatians (II Cor. 2:13, 7:6, 13-14, 8:6, 16, 23, 12:18, Gal. 2:1, 3). He mentioned Silas to the Corinthians (II Cor. 1:19). But does Paul ever send to any of these churches greetings from

Luke? Never. Does he even once mention Luke to them? Never. If Luke had been a close companion of Paul, traveling with him and working with him for nine years throughout Macedonia, Achaia and Asia Minor, would Paul have reflected this somewhere in his letters? And would he not, after such an enduring personal association with Luke, and writing to Luke's Christian friends, have sent greetings from Luke? We judge certainly that he would have. Why does Paul remain silent about Luke when writing to these particular Christians? The only reasonable judgment which we can make is that Luke did not work with Paul in these cities and provinces.

Does Paul indicate that he is acquainted with Luke in any respect? He sends greetings from Luke in two of his letters, once in writing to Philemon and once in writing to the Colossians: (1) "Epaphras, my fellow prisoner in Messiah Jesus, sends greetings to you, and so do Mark, Aristarchus, Demas and Luke my fellow-workers" (Philm. 23-24). (2) "Luke the beloved physician and Demas greet you" (Col. 4:14). Many noteworthy critics insist that Paul did not write Philemon and that he did not write Colossians, which insistence at first sight tends to demolish the acquaintance of Luke and Paul. We are inclined, however, to support the Pauline authorship of these two letters as well as an association between Luke and Paul in Ephesus. This great city was the crossroads and the intellectual center of the first century Christian world. Itinerant apostles, prophets and teachers sooner or later in their travels reached Ephesus, which gave them excellent opportunity to meet and exchange ideas with other itinerants. After working for three years in Arabia, eleven years in Syria and Cilicia, then five and one-half years in Macedonia and Achaia, Paul went to Ephesus 51 A.D. where he stayed for more than three years, motivated in part at least by a desire to have easy access to other Christian workers of the Mediterranean world. Paul probably met Luke in Ephesus. As a tribute to Paul near 90 A.D. the Christians in Ephesus collected Paul's letters, to bring them together for the first time into a compendium. And if by virtue of any reasonable consideration the worthy critics of Paul's letters are right, and Paul did not write Philemon and Colossians, these letters even so reflect information which survived among the Christians of Ephesus, whereupon they still lend support to the acquaintance of Luke and Paul in Ephesus.

Where did Philemon live? In Colossae. Where was Paul living? And assuming that he wrote Philemon and Colossians when did he write them? Paul wrote to Philemon and to the Colossians from prison in Ephesus late 53 or early 54 A.D. Where was Luke who through Paul sends greetings to Philemon and to the Colossians? Luke was certainly in Ephesus and in communication with Paul; at least we would consider it a kind of dishonesty and not in keeping with Paul's character for him to invent these greetings without Luke's request, without Luke's knowledge and in Luke's absence.

Was Luke acquainted personally with Philemon and with the Colossian Christians? We judge beyond any reasonable doubt that he was. We judge further that not only Luke but also all those others who through Paul send greetings--Mark, Aristarchus and Demas--were

16

acquainted with Philemon and with the Colossians in a very personal
way. It would be most unusual for Paul to send greetings from unknown
entities.

How would Luke have made his personal acquaintance with the
Colossians? He would have been in Colossae. He would have met them
prior to the time of Paul's writing. How did Luke get acquainted with
Philemon? He would have met him likewise in Colossae, though he could
have met him in Ephesus. Did Paul and Luke ever travel to Colossae
together? Certainly not before Paul wrote these letters. Paul had
never yet been in Colossae. It is in fact improbable that Paul ever
got there. Luke independently from Paul met the Colossians and
probably became acquainted with Philemon in Colossae. This personal
acquaintance justifies Paul's sending greetings to them from Luke.

Now we return to the question (1): Was Luke a companion of Paul
as Paul worked throughout Macedonia, Achaia and Asia Minor? We must
judge that he was not, that Luke did not work with Paul in establishing
churches in Philippi, Thessalonica, Corinth and Galatia, else Paul
would have sent Luke's greetings to them.

We have no evidence that Paul and Luke ever made any kind of trip
together, no evidence that they ever worked together.

This brings us to our second and earlier question (2): Did Luke
as an eyewitness of activities and events described therein and as a
companion of Paul write The Acts of the Apostles? To this question we
must reply in the negative. To treat extensively The Acts of the
Apostles is not our interest in this work. Our purpose essentially is
to examine Paul according to Paul as he worked among the early
Christians.

As we reconstruct Paul's movements from his letters and as our
understanding of Paul from his letters develops, and as we compare this
reconstruction with The Acts reports on Paul, this comparison with the
information about him as found in The Acts will soon demonstrate that
the author of The Acts had no personal acquaintance with Paul, had only
a meager acquaintance with some of Paul's movements, and could have been
in no way a companion of Paul.

If Luke actually traveled with Paul, worked with him and wrote The
Acts, then he forgot most of the events which actually happened to them
and he invented many things which he never witnessed, things which
never happened. We cannot feature Luke nor any other eyewitness for
that matter having written The Acts of the Apostles. In any case, the
author of The Acts of the Apostles, not being a personal acquaintance
of Paul, could not have been Luke.

No eyewitness account of Paul's life survives. Such an account
was probably never written.

Our earliest information about Paul comes to us from Paul himself
in the letters which he wrote, not as a systematized account of his

life but rather information which comes through sporadically, spontaneously, unpredictably in relatively isolated bits and pieces. We sometimes have difficulty fitting this information into a reasonable chronology. We wish he had told us more. Usually when Paul recounts his own experiences he is refuting opponents or correcting misunderstandings of one kind or another which were generated by his preaching.

When Paul preached the gospel in Thessalonica, Corinth, Galatia and elsewhere did he always communicate clearly to his listeners? Certainly not! Ideas and attitudes were not clearly defined. The whole Christian program was amorphous. He was feeling his way through a maze of new territory as he related Christianity to the gentiles.

Did Paul's listeners always understand accurately what Paul said? Paul's message did not always come through clearly to them, and they were often confused, witness (1) the reaction of some of the Thessalonians to his preaching about the return of Jesus, (2) his complaint that the Corinthians did not understand the meaning and significance of his first letter to them, and complaints of opponents who raised questions about the legitimacy of his claim that he is truly an apostle, and (3) the dichotomy which his preaching created in Galatia: those who because of their impressions of Paul's preaching think that by subscribing to Jewish practices, especially circumcision, they are doing that which will please Paul, as opposed to those who find his gospel of freedom inconsistent with what they regarded to be his approval of Judaism.

In the heat of debate generated between ourselves and others, in defending our sympathies do we tend to exaggerate somewhat our own side in order to accentuate the reasonableness of our position, to vindicate any and all accusations heaped upon us, as if the greater our exaggeration the stronger is our case? Human nature seems so to dispose us. Do emotional pressures lead us to stress the affirmative to the neglect of negative aspects, even though we are well aware of them, negative items which make our case stronger only when we can ignore them? We often tend to assume this attitude, and if we are unable to ignore them we are apt to minimize them. Do we sometimes, in the heat of debate, ridicule our opponent, expecting that this kind of personal insult will somehow make his whole case untenable? This often comes through as a defense mechanism, especially when we are aware that our arguments demonstrate a bit of weakness.

We should not regard Paul as an exception to these tendencies, disputing with enemies, emphasizing his own side to exonerate his case, even subtly ridiculing his enemies or possibly himself, but at the same time we must regard Paul's reports about himself, often casual and unstudied even in the heat of debate, as representing the most reliable, trustworthy, authentic information about him which we have. Did Paul know as much about himself, his own attitudes and activities, probably more, than did his opponents? We would tend to judge so, and certainly he understood himself differently.

In this study we propose to reconstruct the succession of Paul's movements in a reasonable chronological sequence, that is, in as good a chronological order as our resources will allow. We will have to jump about from one letter to another, trying to fit together bits and pieces of information until our task achieves at last a satisfactory degree of completion. Then we will turn our attention to review each of his letters separately, so that what we have learned of Paul's activities will be somewhat reaffirmed and verified. We list his letters according to our judgment in chronological order as follows:

I Thessalonians   50 A.D.   Corinth

(II Thessalonians)   (50 A.D.)   (Corinth)
    (Pauline authorship denied).

I Corinthians   53 or early 54 A.D.   Ephesus
    (Possibly a page from this letter is found in
    II Corinthians 6:14-7:1, referred to in
    I Corinthians 5:9-13).

Philippians   53 or early 54 A.D.   Ephesus

Philemon   54 A.D.   Ephesus
    (Pauline authorship questionable).

Colossians   54 A.D.   Ephesus
    (Pauline authorship questionable).

Ephesians   54 A.D.   Ephesus
    (If Paul wrote this letter he sent it to the
    Laodiceans as referred to in Colossians 4:16,
    possibly a circular letter to the Christians
    of the Lycus river valley. Pauline authorship
    questionable).

II Corinthians   spring 54 A.D.   Ephesus
    (Found in I Corinthians 1:1-16:24).

III Corinthians   54 A.D.   Ephesus
    (Part of this letter is found in II Corin-
    thians 10:1-13:14, referred to in II
    Corinthians 2:4, 7:8,12).

Galatians   summer (July?) 54 A.D.   Ephesus

IV Corinthians   fall (November?) 54 A.D. Macedonia
    (Found in II Corinthians 1:1-6:13, 7:2-9:15).

Romans   55 A.D.   Corinth
    (Sent to Ephesus without chapter 15, sent to
    Rome without chapter 16, and sent to other
    churches without chapters 15 and 16).

(I Timothy)   (100-175 A.D.?)   (unknown)
    (Pauline authorship denied).

(II Timothy)   (100-175 A.D.?)   (unknown)
   (Pauline authorship denied).

(Titus)   (100-175 A.D.?)   (unknown)
   (Pauline authorship denied).

What is the very earliest literary notice, the very earliest bit of information which we have of Paul? He is in the city of Corinth 50 A.D. with Silas and Timothy writing his very first letter, a letter to the Christians in Thessalonica whom he had left just a few weeks earlier. After working approximately two years in Thessalonica he nourished the church to the point where he thought they could carry themselves without him, so he moved on, down to Athens in Achaia. He sent Timothy from Athens back to Thessalonica to get a report for him on the activities of the church.

Why did Paul judge it expedient to send Timothy back to Thessalonica? Somehow he learned that the Thessalonian community during his brief absence was deteriorating and needed his help. The early Christian communities found a cohesion in a host of itinerant workers, spirit filled apostles, prophets and teachers who tramped from community to community, some of them establishing new churches, others nourishing the churches which apostles before them had already established. We do not know how Paul learned that the Thessalonians were swamped with problems, but we are inclined to suspect that the Thessalonians requested an itinerant worker to report to Paul in Athens, or that by chance such a worker met Paul in Athens and reported voluntarily. In any case Paul sent Timothy back to Thessalonica. Paul and Silas meanwhile moved on to Corinth where Timothy, after completing his Thessalonian visit, rejoined them, probably delivered to Paul a letter from the Thessalonians, and reported to Paul on their situation (I Thes. 3:1-6).

The Acts gives a fairly different story: In Thessalonica Paul argued with Jewish people for three sabbaths in the synagogue. After an undue disturbance of the peace Paul, Silas and Timothy were sent away to Beroea by night. In Beroea Paul went to the Jewish synagogue, as he had done in Thessalonica, and, strange reversal, had a very congenial time with them and converted a fair number of Jewish people to believe that Jesus is Messiah. Some Jewish people from Thessalonica then came down to Beroea and stirred up the crowds against them, whereupon Paul went on to Athens. Silas and Timothy remained in Beroea until they got word to join Paul as soon as possible in Athens (17:1-15).

The author of The Acts is a bit confused on the sequence of Paul's movements, which has since served to obscure the facts of Paul's activities in comparison to what Paul tells of himself. He did not know how long Paul actually worked in Thessalonica. He did not know that Paul sent Timothy from Athens back to Thessalonica to get a report on his Thessalonian church. He did not know that Timothy rejoined Paul and Silas in Corinth. The details of The Acts report cannot be supported from the information which Paul gives of his movements in his letters.

Was it expedient for Paul to return immediately to Thessalonica where he would have the advantage of confronting the situation personally? He judged that the situation was not so urgent as all that because he hoped to return to Thessalonica relatively soon anyway. Meanwhile an answer to their letter giving to the Thessalonian church instructions on how they as Christians should conduct themselves through the crises which they faced will serve as a satisfactory substitute for a personal visit.

Is I Thessalonians the very first letter which Paul ever wrote to any of the churches which he founded? It would be rather presumptuous for us to insist in definitive fashion that it is. We would hope that he did write earlier letters, that he corresponded with his churches in Syria and Cilicia. But he probably did not, and if he did such letters have not survived. This emptiness cannot be used as an argument for, nor can it be used as an argument against. From the information now available we must judge that I Thessalonians is his earliest letter as they have been preserved, that it was a new idea to Paul which resulted from his response to a letter which Timothy delivered to him in Corinth from the Thessalonian church, and all his letters as we now have them were written 50 to 55 A.D. All insights which Paul gives about himself and the early Christians are to be found in these letters, near the end of his life. When he wrote I Thessalonians from Corinth 50 A.D. most of his active life as an apostle of Jesus Messiah was past. Only a little more than five years remained. Most of his work was done. He was too busy, possibly too infirm to visit his churches as he wished. Letter writing became a fitting substitute. In addition to the immediate situations which he faced in the churches when he wrote he sometimes reflected back over the years, back over his days in Damascus, in Arabia, again in Damascus, in Jerusalem to visit Peter when he met James, eleven years in Syria and Cilicia, a journey to Jerusalem with Barnabas and back to Antioch of Syria where he confronted Peter during Peter's visit there, and on to Macedonia, Achaia and Asia Minor for nine years where he subsequently spent his last days.

What he tells us about himself, all the information which he gives about his life, is in retrospect, a glance backward at things which happened to him twenty-five years ago, twenty-four, twenty-three, twenty, fifteen, ten years ago, or perhaps incidents which occurred within the last few months, understood by him now and interpreted by him from the viewpoint of one whose years have been difficult, whose apostolic calling has been vindicated not only by his having acquired approval from the Jerusalem nucleus but also by the several churches which he established and by his loyalty to the request of the Jerusalem pillars that he take collections from his churches for the Jerusalem poor. His years of service are mostly behind him. Those which are left are to be brought very shortly and unexpectedly to an untimely end.

How many years was Paul active preaching the gospel to gentiles before he wrote his first letter? Twenty-one years from late 29 A.D. when the risen Jesus appeared in him in Damascus and clarified to him his purpose of preaching the gospel to gentiles until 50 A.D. when he scribbled out, possibly dictated his Thessalonian letter, Paul spent twenty-one years, his first twenty-one years as an apostle in the Christian arena, in literary silence. During this whole time there is an empty space, a total literary void; and so far as we can determine Paul wrote no letters to his churches during these twenty-one years, at least none which have survived. He wrote nothing about himself, except for what seeps through in his letters, and no one wrote anything about him.

This is true not only of Paul and his life but also of the life of the church at large. The early Christians did not write literature. Why did they not produce any written accounts of Jesus? Why did they not keep a written account of activities and occurrences within the church? They were not academicians. They did not need to write books. They already had a book, The Law and the Prophets, to which they would add nothing and from which they would subtract nothing. Everything God wanted them to know was written therein. Anything which God did not write into this book was hardly worth knowing. But better still Jesus will return soon. If Jesus is going to return today, well then tomorrow, before the week is out, certainly before the year is up, well then certainly within our own lifetimes, there is no need to write books. Paul's letter to the Thessalonians is the very first morsel of Christian literature which has survived. All other Christian literature which we have in the New Testament and elsewhere appeared after Paul's letter to the Thessalonians in 50 A.D. Paul certainly did not understand, when he wrote to the Thessalonians, that he was heralding a new era within Christianity, an era of Christian literature, nor did he have the slightest anticipation that one day this little production would be included within a collection of Christian literature which Christians would regard as sacred scripture.

PART II

PAUL THE APOSTLE

PAUL THE APOSTLE

Where was Paul born and where did he grow up? We do not know.
He makes no mention of birthplace, no mention of parents, no mention
of boyhood home, no mention of schooling, no mention of the direction
of early professional interests.

A tradition recorded in The Acts of the Apostles makes Tarsus of
Cilicia his birthplace, and Jerusalem the city where he grew up (9:11,
30, 11:25, 21:39, 22:3). The fact of the matter is, we do not know
where Paul was born and where he grew up.

As he poured out his thoughts and feelings to the Galatians Paul
makes one reference to his pre-earthly days, if we can speak of such
as having days, an insistence that God set him apart for the task of
preaching the gospel before he was born (Gal. 1:15). Paul's disposition might well be an echo of Jeremiah: ". . . before you were born
I consecrated you; I appointed you a prophet to the nations" (Jer. 1:5).
We can regard Paul's outlook as somewhat like that reflected by
Sophocles in Oedipus Rex, that from birth, even before birth, God has
in mind a destiny for us to fulfill and it is absolutely impossible
for us ultimately to do otherwise. We might deliberately rebel and
frustrate God's plans by going in the opposite direction as did king
Oedipus, and as did Paul when he fought against God by persecuting
Christians, but such a rebellion can be at best only temporary. God
will appropriately and in due time step into the picture, take charge,
and use us to fulfill his destiny. Paul judged that this is exactly
what God did to him. God assigned him before he was born to the task
of preaching the gospel of Messiah to the nations, and there was no
way he could avoid this destiny.

Paul insists that he was descended from Abraham, born a Hebrew of
the people of Israel, of the tribe of Benjamin, and that he was a
Pharisee (Phil. 3:5). He passes over his babyhood with a singular but
emphatic reference to his eighth day circumcision. He makes no mention
of childhood, youth and early manhood unless by chance his adhesion to
the law as a Pharisee, his righteousness under the law as blameless
which means he omitted nothing however trivial, and his advancement in
Judaism as beyond that of many of his own age among his people have
foundations in these earlier days of his life (Phil. 3:6, II Cor. 11:22,
Gal. 1:14).

Paul's report on his adhesion to the law as a Pharisee was
adequate for the author of The Acts to make Paul a student of Gamaliel,
the great Pharisee and teacher of the law (22:3).

25

Was Paul a persecutor of Christians? He gives the impression that
he persecuted the church of God violently and tried to destroy it,
stressing the fact that his zeal for the traditions of his religious
heritage generated this disposition within him (I Cor. 15:9, Phil. 3:6,
Gal. 1:13, 23). He doubtless thought at the time that this served to
accumulate for him a great degree of religious merit, that he was doing
God a tremendous favor and that it guaranteed God's favor toward him.
He tended to be a bit complacent for his inhumane achievement.

What changed the course of Paul's attitudes and activities? The
risen Jesus appeared in him in Damascus and clarified his assignment,
the task which God had in mind for him before he was born, and this
effected an about face (Gal. 1:15-16, I Cor. 15:5-8). Paul condemns
his previous abuse of Christians, and he turned to promulgate that
which he previously despised.

By 90 A.D. the story of Paul's persecution against Christians had
gained some rather inflated dimensions. When Paul enters the stage in
The Acts of the Apostles he is living in Jerusalem, ruthless and blood-
thirsty, breathing out threats and murder against the Christians in
Jerusalem, approving of and officiating at the martyrdom of Stephen,
then entering house after house, dragging men and women off to prison
(7:58, 8:1, 3, 9:1).

Paul gives a somewhat different story. Where was he living when
the resurrected Jesus appeared in him? We get the idea easily from
his letter to the Galatians that he was living in Damascus, Damascus
was his home, he had never been in Jerusalem before this time, and he
made his very first trip to Jerusalem three years after the risen Jesus
appeared in him in Damascus (Gal. 1:18). Paul's persecuting activites,
whatever they might have been, could not have occurred in Jerusalem.
Not living in Jerusalem, he did not breathe out threats and murder
against the church in Jerusalem, and he did not approve of and officiate
at the martyrdom of Stephen.

According to The Acts of the Apostles, after devastating the
church of Jerusalem Paul went to the high priest and requested letters
to the synagogues of Damascus giving him permission to root out Christians there, arrest them and transport them to Jerusalem for trial
(9:1-2).

Would Paul, who was a Pharisee and attached therefore to the synagogue, go to the high priest who was chief of the Sadducees and request
of him any such letters? The high priest would regard this certainly
as a most unusual request. Did the high priest who was the major
religious functionary in the temple in Jerusalem have any jurisdiction
over the synagogues whether in Jerusalem, Damascus or elsewhere?
Did the high priest have any authority to issue such letters, even if
Paul did request them, and would he have issued them? He had no such

26

authority and the nature of his position would have required him to refuse any such request from Paul or from anyone else. It would have been impossible for Paul to get any such letters from the high priest in Jerusalem.

Nevertheless the author of The Acts, unaware that Paul had never yet been in Jerusalem, depicts Paul in route from Jerusalem to Damascus with a retinue of officials, carrying letters from the high priest in Jerusalem to introduce him to the synagogues with the express assignment of liquidating Christians.

As Paul and his cohorts approached Damascus something unexpected and unpredictable happened. A light flashed from heaven striking him blind, he fell to the ground, Jesus spoke to him and told him to go into the city where he would receive further instructions. He was led blind into the city to the house of Judas on Straight Street, was without sight for three days, until Ananias guided by the Spirit laid his hands on him, scales fell from his eyes, he regained his sight, ate food for the first time in three days, was baptized, and went into the synagogues not to arrest Christians but to preach Messiah (9:3-19). Tradition regards this on the road to Damascus experience as the conversion of Paul.

The author of The Acts of the Apostles records Paul's on the road to Damascus experience three times: 9:3-19, 22:6-16, 26:12-18. We cannot read these three accounts soberly without being impressed by their apparent inconsistencies.

In 9:4, 7 Paul fell to the ground while the men who were traveling with him stood speechless; in 22:7 Paul fell to the ground with no mention of the action of those who were with him; and in 26:14 all of them, Paul and those who were with him, fell to the ground.

Those traveling with Paul heard the voice in 9:7 but saw nothing; they did not hear the voice but they did see the light in 22:9; and Paul only is mentioned as hearing the voice in 26:14.

In the first account, 9:6, the voice instructed Paul to go into the city where he will be told what to do; in the second account, 22:10, in response to the inquiry "What shall I do?" the voice instructed him to go into the city where he will be told what to do; and in the third account, 26:16, the voice instructed Paul what to do on the very spot where he was struck down.

The author of The Acts was unable to tell this story consistently three times over.

What does Paul have to say in his letters of the on the road to Damascus experience? Nothing. Paul is unaware of any great cataclytic conversion experience in route to Damascus as reported about him near 95 A.D. by the author of The Acts (9:3-19, 22:16-16, 26:12-18).

27

Paul tells an entirely different story about these matters, and we should do well to listen soberly to his voice. Since he was living in Damascus and in fact had never been in Jerusalem he was never in route from Jerusalem to Damascus for any purpose whatever, and certainly not to liquidate Christians. Paul never mentions such a conversion experience, is unaware that he was ever converted in such a manner. He believed that God had set him apart to preach the gospel of Messiah to gentiles before he was born, and the appearance of the resurrected Jesus in him was merely a clarification of this assignment (Gal. 1:15-17, I Cor. 15:8).

When did Paul identify himself with the Christian movement? Probably 29 A.D. How do we arrive at this date? By establishing (1) the date for Jesus' execution, and by determining (2) how long Jesus continued to appear after he was resurrected.

(1) When was Jesus executed? The only bit of information which we have in response to this question suggests that Jesus was crucified at the Passover in the spring of 28 A.D., a conversation between Jesus and some Jewish people in Jerusalem which is found in the 100-130 A.D. Gospel according to John 2:19-20. Jesus announced to his adversaries, "Destroy this temple and in three days I will raise it up", using the word temple to refer to his own physical body (from the viewpoint of the early Christians man's body is the temple of God) and of his resurrection. They misunderstood Jesus' implication as they stood there in the shadow of the temple in Jerusalem; temple called to their minds the Herodian temple, and they replied, "This temple has been a-building for forty-six years. . ."

When did this conversation occur? Herod began the construction of the temple, or had it begun, in 20 B.C. Forty-six years a-building (it was never really completed) added to 20 B.C. would place the date for this particular conversation between Jesus and his associates 27 A.D.

Did this conversation occur before or after the 27 A.D. Passover? It appears to have occurred very soon after the Passover.

Was Jesus crucified on the Passover following this conversation? Trusting in the reliability of the fourth evangelist John it is fair to judge that he was, and this means that the 28 A.D. Passover is established as the date of Jesus' execution. There is no evidence which suggests any other date. No Roman record of the event has been found: no record of his trial, no execution order, no death certificate, no burial certificate.

(2) Paul's commitment to the movement, simultaneous with the clarification of his apostolic assignment, had to occur within that period of time when the resurrected Jesus was making his appearances. Reflecting back over twenty-five years Paul enumerated those appearances: Peter, the twelve, more than five-hundred brothers at one time, James, all the apostles, and "last of all as to an apostle untimely born he appeared also in me" (I Cor. 15:5-8, compare Gal. 1:16).

Did Paul consider the appearance of Jesus in him to be the same as were those appearances in others? Indeed he did. Was Jesus' appearance in Paul the very last of the series? Paul insisted that it certainly was.

How long after Jesus was resurrected did he continue his appearances? The tradition which was held by the Ophites, by the disciples of Valentinius, recorded in the second century Ascension of Isaiah, and held extensively by the early Christians at large attributed to these appearances a span of eighteen months. Relying on this tradition and on Paul's claim that the risen Jesus appeared last of all in him we easily judge that Paul would have had to identify with the messianic movement a year and a half after Jesus was crucified.

The Passover of 28 A.D. when Jesus was executed plus eighteen months during which Jesus made his appearances finally to appear in Paul equals late 29 A.D. as the time when Paul identified himself with the messianic movement.

This date, late 29 A.D., the time when the risen Jesus appeared in Paul in Damascus and clarified the purpose which God had in mind for him before he was born, is very important. It signifies to us that sometime during this brief span of one and one-half years some devotees of Jesus had visited the synagogues in Damascus and convinced some of the Jewish people that Jesus is Messiah. How long did it take these Christian evangelists to get there? One month? Six months? One year? We do not really know, but are inclined to judge that soon after the execution of Jesus they moved east of the Jordan river to Pella, then north to Damascus, confident that the kingdom would begin east of the Jordan as Isaiah had reported (Is. 9:1), and that they were thereby fulfilling their role in establishing that kingdom, continuing the work which Jesus had begun.

For how long and to what extent did Paul persecute Christians? Any persecution in which he indulged would have occurred after Christian believers were established in the synagogue in Damascus and before the late 29 A.D. appearance of the risen Jesus in him in Damascus, probably less than one year and maybe for only one or two months. Paul mentions it in three of his letters--I Corinthians, Philippians and Galatians-- and he wrote all three of these letters in 54 A.D., that is, twenty-five years post eventum. And no one, not even Paul, wrote an eyewitness agenda from which we can get the details. We have no reliable description of his activities in the role of persecutor. The author of The Acts tried to fill in the missing parts, but he allowed his imagination to carry him far beyond the limits of reality.

Did Judaism have an organization with employed persecutors against multiple and varied religious points of view? Certainly not. Was Judaism aggressive in either desire or attempt to destroy any other religion? Never. Were the Jewish people in Damascus or elsewhere aware of Paul's persecuting activities? Certainly not either as mentioned by Paul or as described by the author of The Acts, and if they had been aware of such they would neither sanction nor approve.

29

Paul's persecution of the church could well have been essentially a personal mental disposition, a self appointment, nothing more than a few verbal flailings, tongue lashing exchanges. In the synagogues the people expressed themselves freely, and Paul's backward glance at his synagogue activities after twenty-five years, his verbal attacks on messianic believers in Jesus, could well set in his mind as occasions of persecution. But after twenty-five years they could also serve another purpose for him, that is, enhance the effectiveness of his preaching among those converts who accepted his message at first with a degree of reluctance.

But 29 A.D. is important further because it is our beginning point with Paul. Our chronology of Paul's activities begin with this date. All of Paul's following activities relate back to it.

What did the appearance of the risen Jesus signify to Paul? He regarded it as a positive awakening to his Christian commitment, a move toward the perfection of what had always been his motivation. It was not something new and different, but rather it was a fulfillment of the purpose which God had in mind for him before he was born (Gal. 1:15), a destiny which it would be impossible for him ultimately to resist. But its implications went even further.

Who were the two kingpins of the Jerusalem church? Peter and James. Peter was very close to Jesus during his ministry in Galilee. After Jesus was resurrected he appeared first in Peter. But who was James? James was a brother of Jesus who reportedly scoffed at Jesus during his earthly ministry. This disposition changed when the resurrected Jesus appeared also in him, a change reflected in the tradition that James repented from his previous disposition by praying in the temple until his knees became calloused like the knees of a camel. In any case James became the chief pillar of the Jerusalem nucleus of Christians. The appearance of the resurrected Jesus in Peter and later in James accorded to both a certain priority within the Jerusalem church.

What judgment did Paul make about the appearance of Jesus in him? Did not the appearance of the risen Jesus in Paul enroll him somehow as equivalent in the Christian community and deserving of status equivalent to that of the pillars of the Jerusalem church, that is, Peter, James and John? It could mean certainly no less than this to him. But he must overcome one stigma, namely, he must convince Peter, James and John that the resurrected Jesus indeed appeared in him by virtue of which he, Paul, deserves status in the Jerusalem church equal to them.

Did Paul go to Jerusalem immediately to claim his spiritual birthright? No. Where did he go? He went away into Arabia, later returned to Damascus, and after a total of three years had passed he went to Jerusalem to visit Peter for fifteen days (Gal. 1:15-18).

The author of The Acts was not fully acquainted with the details, unaware that Paul preached in Arabia for three years, unaware that after this period of three years Paul made his very first trip to Jerusalem,

unaware that on this very first visit to Jerusalem he stayed with P
for fifteen days, met James, but remained unknown to the churches i
Judea.

Paul reports that he was lowered in a basket through a window
the wall at Damascus, whereupon he escaped the governor under king
Aretas (Aretas IV reigned over Syria 9 A.D. to 40 A.D.) who guarde
city in order to seize him (II Cor. 11:32-33). When did this occu
Did it occur immediately before he went away into Arabia for three
years? Or did it occur after his three years in Arabia as a prel
his first trip to Jerusalem? Paul does not specify. We can only
cate with the very strongest degree of probability that it relate
one of these two occasions, and that it occurred sometime within
years after the risen Jesus appeared in Paul, and it occurred mor
probably just before his trip to Jerusalem.

The author of The Acts (9:22-26) gives a different story.
Paul regained his sight he appeared in the synagogues in Damascu
that Jesus is the Messiah. How did the Jewish people in Damasc
to Paul's ability to prove that Jesus is Messiah? They were con
plotted to kill him, watched the city gates day and night to app
him. Paul learned of the plot and the disciples lowered him dow
the wall in a basket by night so he could escape and return to J
lem.

The author of The Acts did not know that it was the govern
wanted to seize Paul, and was also unaware that Paul was let do
wall through a window. He is not fully acquainted with the det
this occasion, but was stampeded by his enthusiasm to show how
suffered persistently at the hands of the Jewish people. He se
be more vindictive toward the Jewish people for their persecuti
Paul, than toward Paul for his program to liquidate Christians.

Paul knows nothing of a Jewish plot to kill him.

Three years after God revealed his Son in him Paul went
salem.

> Then after three years I went up to Jerusalem to visit Ce
> and remained with him fifteen days. But I saw none of th
> other apostles except James the Lord's brother. (In what
> am writing to you, before God, I do not lie!) Then I wer
> into the regions of Syria and Cilicia. And I was still r
> known by sight to the churches of Messiah in Judea; they
> only heard it said, "He who once persecuted us is now pr
> ing the faith he once tried to destroy" (Gal. 1:18-23).

This was Paul's first trip to Jerusalem, three years after th
Jesus appeared in him, late 32 A.D., possibly early 33 A.D. (
A.D. is still within that period which can be referred to as
three years").

31

Paul had never been in Jerusalem before. He was unknown to the Christians in Jerusalem, and he was unknown to the Christians throughout Judea. They had heard of him. They talked about him. But they did not know him either before this trip to Jerusalem or during his visit there. He visited Peter for fifteen days during which time he met James the brother of Jesus. But he remained unknown by sight to the church in Jerusalem and to the churches of Judea, and he continued to remain unknown by sight to them, they did not know him personally, for another eleven years. After working for eleven years in Syria and Cilicia Paul went to Jerusalem a second time, this trip with Barnabas and Titus, his first personal acquaintance with the Jerusalem Christians. All this means that Paul had been preaching the gospel for fourteen years before the Jerusalem Christians, exclusive of Peter and James, even made their very first acquaintance with him. We must rely on the relative accuracy of Paul's own words, which tell us loudly and clearly that at no time was he a persecutor of Christians in Jerusalem.

The author of The Acts (9:26-30) takes Paul back to Jerusalem very soon after his "conversion" experience, after he escapes from some Jewish people who plotted to kill him. Back in Jerusalem what did Paul try to do? He attempted to join the disciples, those whom he had just a few weeks earlier harrassed and devastated, but they were skeptical of his unusual and unprecedented reversal, did not trust him. Barnabas took him to the apostles, related to them his experience in route to Damascus, whereupon they received Paul into the Jerusalem community. He preached among them so boldly and convincingly that the Hellenists sought to kill him, whereupon the brothers hustled him off to Caesarea and sent him on to Tarsus.

The author of The Acts is unaware that Paul lived in Damascus and that he worked in Arabia for three years before making his first trip to Jerusalem.

Which account are we to regard as more accurate? Paul's account of his activities or The Acts account? Was Paul capable of reporting accurately on his own movements? We would judge so, and we would suspect that the author of The Acts had inaccurate information; all of which means that Paul was not a persecutor of Christians in Jerusalem, he did not go to Damascus to arrest Christians, he was not "converted" in a cataclytic manner, he did not subsequently preach Messiah in the synagogues in Damascus, Jewish people in Damascus did not plot to kill him, he did not go back to Jerusalem immediately after his "conversion", was not held in suspicion by the Christians in Jerusalem, Barnabas did not take him to the apostles and interpose for him, Paul did not preach with such vigor that he aroused hostility from hellenistic Jewish people who endangered his life, and the Christian community of Jerusalem did not send him off to Tarsus.

What then did Paul really do after the resurrected Jesus clarified his assignment? Did he set out for Jerusalem? Certainly not! He went away into Arabia and preached for three years before he made his very

first trip to Jerusalem, and he used his preaching in Arabia as evidence for the fact that he did not receive from Peter or James or any of the other apostles in Jerusalem the gospel which he was preaching because he preached it for three years in Arabia before he even met any of the apostles.

Why did Paul make this first trip to Jerusalem? The appearance of the risen Jesus in Paul gave him something in common with both Peter and James. His report to Peter of his experience of the risen Jesus in Damascus seemed to carry overtones. Paul went to Jerusalem to request of Peter status in the church equivalent to that of the Jerusalem pillars.

Could Peter and James appreciate Jesus' appearances in themselves and others in and around Galilee, the area of his earthly activities? This was indeed meaningful to both of them. But what was their reaction to Paul's claim that Jesus appeared in him over in Damascus? This was somewhat far-fetched. They were not fully congenial to Paul's ambitions.

Their considerations went further, however, than a mere matter of Paul's ambitions. With the church still in its infancy, trying to identify itself and find its way through the maze of its Jewish inheritance, what problem generated more disturbance, caused more consternation among them, than any other? Their relations with the Pharisees. A fair sized bloc of Pharisees had assumed the messianic faith but continued in effect being Pharisees. Was Paul a Pharisee? He certainly was, extremely loyal to Pharisaism, and he never really ceased being one. Did Peter and James suspect that Paul as a Pharisee would be an agitator of sorts and only serve to multiply their problems with the Pharisaic Christians? They probably did.

Is Christianity different from Pharisaism? The Pharisees who became Christians simply added to their Pharisaism the belief that Jesus is Messiah. But the Jerusalem pillars understood it a bit differently, drew some lines of demarcation and understood the Pharisaic Christians as never having fully embraced Christianity.

How many covenants did God give? The Jerusalem Christians were convinced that God revealed his covenant through Abraham, and that he spoke singularly throughout the ages, revealing this same covenant again and again through Isaac, Jacob, Moses, Joshua, David, Amos, Hosea, Isaiah, Micah, Jeremiah, Ezekiel, in fact through all his prophets from Abraham onwards, a covenant which was in fact a foreannouncement of Jesus and which was at last clarified through Jesus' appearance on earth. God's word is singular and consistent, eternal and unchanging, and this means that the covenant which God revealed through Moses is in reality the very same covenant which God revealed first through Abraham, then subsequently through all the prophets, at last clarified through Jesus. God has given only one covenant.

To whom has God given this covenant? God has given this covenant to his people, whom he has chosen. The Jerusalem Christians regarded themselves as Israel, God's chosen people. They were convinced that they were the custodians of this covenant of God.

Does this covenant have anything to do with the law of Moses? Certainly not! It is unrelated to and it has no kinship whatever to the law which tradition attributed to Moses.

Peter and James were having problems in Jerusalem with Pharisees who had become Christians. What seemed to be the source of these problems? The Pharisees had an attachment to the law of Moses, which they regarded erroneously as God's covenant through Moses. They refused to forfeit this attachment. They insisted that one finds perfection in Christianity through the route of the Mosaic institution.

Did Paul understand this conflict? He seems to have understood it quite well. He regarded it somewhat as an offense to his Pharisaic heritage. What did Paul do, with all due respect toward both Christianity and Pharisaism, to resolve this conflict? He offered a solution to Christianity's conflict with Pharisaism by inventing his theory of two covenants: (1) a covenant which God gave through Moses for the Jewish people, and (2) a covenant which God gave through Jesus for Christians. The Jerusalem pillars regarded Paul's theory of two covenants as a forthright denial of the changelessness of God's eternal word.

What did Paul's theory of two covenants suggest to the Christians in Jerusalem? Paul's insistence on a Mosaic covenant for Jewish people suggested to the Jerusalem pillars that he is moreso a Pharisee than a Christian, that in association with Jerusalem Pharisaic Christians he would only give them additional problems, and they were probably right. Paul claimed to receive his Christian disposition through revelation, which put him in a position of no compromise. He was unwilling to forfeit his Pharisaism.

Paul went to Jerusalem, by virtue of the fact that the risen Jesus appeared in him in Damascus, to acquire a coveted position in the Jerusalem circle, status equivalent to that of the pillars. Peter and James refused to grant him this recognition.

What can Paul do now? He turned his attention to the regions of Syria and Cilicia (Gal. 1:21) to preach the gospel of Messiah among the gentiles.

What do we know of Paul's activities in Syria and Cilicia? We know that he worked there for eleven years (Gal. 1:21-2:1), from late 32 A.D. or possible early 33 A.D. until late 43 A.D. How many churches did he establish there? We do not know. In what cities in Syria and Cilicia did he establish churches? We do not know. Paul relates one incident which, in view of the chronology of his itinerary, we can relate to his experiences in Syria and Cilicia, his visit to the third heaven, as he reports:

I know a man in Messiah who fourteen years ago was caught up to the third heaven--whether in the body or out of the body I do not know, God knows. And I know that this man was caught up into Paradise--whether in the body or out of the body I do not know, God knows--and he heard things that cannot be told, which man may not utter (II Cor. 12:2-3).

Paul wrote this to the Corinthians in 54 A.D. If we understand literally this very unusual experience which he claims we would place it in 40 A.D., which was near the end of his eleven years in Syria and Cilicia. But Paul could well have used "fourteen years ago" symbolically to refer to the time span between two very important events in his life, (1) the appearance of the risen Jesus in him and (2) his recognition by Peter, James and John as an apostle to the gentiles. And if he had these in mind his third heaven experience relates to the appearance of the risen Jesus in him in Damascus.

In the very same letter to the Corinthians, II Corinthians 11:22-27, Paul made some further reflections into his past:

> Are they Hebrews? So am I. Are they Israelites? So am I. Are they descendents of Abraham? So am I. Are they servants of Messiah? I am a better one--I am talking like a madman--with far greater labors, far more imprisonments, with countless beatings, and often near death. Five times I have received at the hands of the Jewish people the forty lashes less one. Three times I have been shipwrecked; a night and a day I have been adrift at sea; on frequent journeys, in danger from rivers, danger from robbers, danger from my own people, danger from gentiles, danger in the city, danger in the wilderness, danger at sea, danger from false brothers; in toil and hardship, through many a sleepless night, in hunger and thirst, often without food, in cold and exposure.

When did all of these things happen to Paul? Certainly they had to happen to him before 54 A.D. when he wrote of them to the Corinthians, which means that they had to happen to him somewhere in relation to his activities in Damascus, Arabia, Jerusalem, Syria, Cilicia, Philippi, Thessalonica, Athens, Corinth, Ephesus and Galatia.

Where was Paul when he endured far more imprisonments than his adversaries (II Cor. 11:23)? He writes of his shameful treatment in Philippi (I Thes. 2:2), but he does not specify exactly what was his problem there. There was no need for him to specify because both the Philippians and the Thessalonians knew the details. He was imprisoned in Philippi, as his letter to the Philippians later reveals: ". . . engaged in the same conflict which you saw and now hear to be mine" (Phil. 1:30). Paul writes these words to the Philippians from prison in Ephesus, and he identifies his situation with that which happened to him in Philippi. His imprisonments in Philippi and in Ephesus are the only occasions which we can relate to the numerous abuses which he reviews in II Corinthians 11:22-27.

Where was Paul when he endured countless beatings, receiving five times at the hands of Jewish people forty lashes less one (II Cor. 11:24)? We do not know. Such beatings usually resulted from disputes between two Jewish men, and any man in dispute with another who in court is found guilty can be according to Jewish law sentenced by the

35

judge to a beating in the judge's presence, the number of lashes commensurate with the offense (Deut. 25:1). If Paul received thirty-nine lashes on five different occasions he would have been found guilty in court of five different offenses in five different disputes. Thirty-nine lashes, the number which Paul reports, indicate that the offenses were regarded by the judges as quite serious. But Paul does not identify the places where he received these punishments.

Where was Paul on three different occasions when he was beaten with Roman rods (II Cor. 11:25)? We do not know. Where was he when one time he was stoned (II Cor. 11:25)? We do not know. Where was Paul when three times he was shipwrecked (II Cor. 11:25)? We do not know. Paul makes no reference elsewhere to any of these events, gives no details in his other letters, in a way by which we can identify them as such. Had they occurred to him in Philippi or Thessalonica, Athens or Corinth, Ephesus or Galatia, that is, within the periphery of his experiences with these Christians, it seems that somewhere in his letters to them he would have made at the very least a casual reference, an indication would have filtered through, as did his imprisonments in Philippi and Ephesus.

The author of The Acts of the Apostles offers no additional enlightenment. He fairly well limits Paul's activities to those communities either (1) to which Paul wrote letters, or (2) which Paul mentioned in his letters: Damascus, Antioch of Syria, Galatia (with which he was not acquainted geographically), Troas, Philippi, Thessalonica, Athens, Corinth, Ephesus, Jerusalem, Rome. He goes beyond these places (1) by taking Paul and Barnabas throughout the island of Cyprus (probably because he was influenced by the tradition that Barnabas preached in Cyprus), (2) in relating Paul's activities in Beroea (about which he has erroneous details), and (3) in having Paul imprisoned in Jerusalem, Caesarea and Rome.

By 95 A.D. the Christians in Ephesus paid a great tribute to Paul by collecting his letters into a compendium, and made them more easily accessible for the Christian world. The author of The Acts, however, demonstrates that he had no acquaintance with them, had never read them.

He has Paul stoned by the people in Lystra (16:23, 22:23-30, 33, 24:27, 28:16), a city which Paul never visited; beaten by Roman rods and imprisoned in Philippi (16:22-24), and his account is more fabulous than real; and shipwrecked only once, near the island of Malta (27:23-28:1). That shipwreck in the chronology of The Acts account of Paul's activities occurred on his trip to Rome as a prisoner, which means that it would have occurred several years after Paul wrote II Corinthians in 54 A.D., and could in no way add any clarification to Paul's account in II Corinthians 11:25.

The author of The Acts has unreliable information, possibly invented these details including his report on Paul's imprisonment in Philippi, and is in fact unacquainted with any details about the incidents which Paul specified in II Corinthians 11:22-27.

36

Paul writes of these misfortunes as if he is reflecting back on a more distant past. Do his recollections of these abuses, except for his imprisonments in Philippi and Ephesus, relate back to things which happened to him while he was in Syria and Cilicia? Our inability to pinpoint them as having occurred in Philippi or Thessalonica, Athens or Corinth, Ephesus or Galatia suggests that several of these occasions of maltreatment might well have occurred to him during his eleven years in Syria and Cilicia. Were they occasions of embarrassment to the Jerusalem Christians? And could they have been incidents which the Jerusalem pillars discussed with Paul when he made his second trip to Jerusalem? We are unable to answer such questions effectively.

Paul reports a second trip to Jerusalem, "after fourteen years", with Barnabas and Titus (Gal. 2:1). His language is not clear as we would like at this point. Is Paul speaking of fourteen years after the resurrected Jesus appeared in him, or is he speaking of fourteen years after his first trip to Jerusalem? He is probably using the time when the risen Jesus appeared in him in Damascus as the base for both these statements, (1) "after three years" (Gal. 1:18) and (2) "after fourteen years" (Gal. 2:1), which means that he worked alone preaching the gospel and establishing churches in Syria and Cilicia for eleven years and then went to Jerusalem with Barnabas and Titus (late 29 A.D. plus fourteen years) in late 43 A.D. Early 44 A.D. is within that time period which could be referred to as "after fourteen years", whereupon Paul could have made his second journey to Jerusalem with Barnabas and Titus in early 44 A.D.

We do not know how Barnabas got into this picture. According to the account related by the author of The Acts the Jerusalem church sent him to take charge of the gentile Christian movement in Antioch, and he went to Tarsus, located Paul, and subsequently Paul and Barnabas went together to Jerusalem to carry charitable contributions from Antioch (11:22, 25-30), then at a still later date attended together the Jerusalem Council (15:1-35).

What circumstances prompted Paul's second trip to Jerusalem (Gal. 2:1)? His eleven years of preaching the gospel in Syria and Cilicia created some problems, generating a situation which was somewhat disturbing to the Jerusalem Christians. What was this situation? We can only surmise. Paul faced the problem of personal allegiance to Pharisaism. When brought face to face with the necessity of distinguishing his Christianity from his Pharisaism Paul held onto both Pharisaism and Christianity in a style somewhat different from the Jerusalem Pharisaic Christians who insisted on a singular covenant revealed through Moses, and in a style different from the Jerusalem Christians who insisted on a singular covenant revealed repeatedly throughout the ages through all the prophets finally to be clarified through Jesus. The Jerusalem community, dominated by James, claimed a certain primacy, the right to direct, to give instructions which the churches, even the gentile churches, could not disregard. Paul went to Jerusalem, his second trip to Jerusalem, fourteen years after the risen Jesus appeared

37

in him in Damascus, with Barnabas and Titus, to discuss with the pillars of the church the gospel which he was preaching among gentiles in Syria and Cilicia, and to benefit from whatever instruction they could give him.

While Paul claimed to receive his gospel by way of revelation from the risen Jesus, his teachings did not harmonize with the impressions which the Jerusalem apostles traced back to Jesus while he was with them in person. With all due respect to Paul the Jerusalem Christians must find a way to correct Paul's errors and especially his error about two covenants which he was preaching in Syria and Cilicia. So in late 43 A.D., possibly early 44 A.D., Barnabas under the auspices of the Jerusalem nucleus went to Antioch, located Paul and invited him to visit the pillars in Jerusalem.

How does The Acts explain this occasion? It uses it to bring Paul onto the stage and into the floodlights of gentile Christianity.

Following the martyrdom of Stephen persecution broke out against the Christians in Jerusalem. Many of them left Jerusalem and traveled as far as Phoenicia, Cyprus and Antioch preaching the gospel but they limited their preaching to Jewish people (11:19).

Meanwhile, after his conversion near Damascus, Paul returned to Jerusalem. He wanted to join the disciples. They were afraid of him. Barnabas convinced the apostles to accept him. Paul disputed with the Hellenists. They sought to kill him. The brothers learned of their design, transported Paul to Caesarea and sent him off to Tarsus (9:26-30).

Others of the itinerants, Jewish Christians native of Cyprus and Cyrene, apparently numbering among those who dispersed from Jerusalem, came to Antioch. They preached to gentiles. A great number were converted. News of this reached Jerusalem. The Jerusalem church sent Barnabas to Antioch to supervise this phenomenon. Barnabas was pleased with what he saw among the Antioch Christians. He then went to Tarsus, located Paul, brought him to Antioch. They taught a large company of people for a whole year, then carried charitable relief to the Christians in Jerusalem (11:20-30).

Paul seems to be unaware of all this. The Jerusalem church sent Barnabas north, possibly to Antioch, to find Paul and bring him to Jerusalem. Paul made this trip with Barnabas and Titus. There is no reason, as Paul tells the story, for us to judge that Barnabas supervised the gentile Christian venture in Antioch, that he sought out Paul in Tarsus, took him to Antioch where they worked together teaching a large company of people for a whole year, and then went to Jerusalem to carry gifts from the Antioch Christians to the Jerusalem Christians.

Would Paul have been on the defensive upon receiving such an invitation from Barnabas? If he should reject Barnabas' invitation would he be in defiance of the Jerusalem pillars? How would such defiance expose him before the whole church? Would the churches soon learn of his discountenance? Would they regard his arrogance with disdain? Would he be exposed unfavorably? Would it place Paul in a position of risking alienation not only from the Jerusalem community forever but also from his own churches in Syria and Cilicia? Eleven years earlier Peter and James had rejected him. Was Paul still carrying smouldering resentments against Peter and James? We think that he was, and that he carried them throughout his life (Gal. 2:6), but he subjected them long enough to agree, though with inward reluctance, to accompany Barnabas to Jerusalem and work with Barnabas until he got what he could interpret as apostolic approval, a prize which he failed to acquire eleven years earlier. Had he long since learned that apostolic approval would be very advantageous for him, in fact a very valuable asset to him in his work among the gentiles? While in route to Jerusalem did Barnabas propose that he and Paul combine forces and work together in the gentile arena?

When Paul reached Jerusalem with Barnabas and Titus the pillars were extremely pleased that Paul and Barnabas had agreed to work together as a team. Paul answered to the pillars, however, concerning his activities in Syria and Cilicia, as he had preached throughout his eleven years in Syria and Cilicia: if one is Jewish by birth, he may subscribe to the Mosaic covenant without adding anything to or taking anything from his Christian commitments, then go on to adhere to the Christian covenant. But what of the gentile who is converted to Christianity? The gentile convert may by-pass the Mosaic covenant and cling only to the covenant through Jesus.

By insisting that Jewish people should honor the Mosaic covenant and in general abide by their birth status Paul was giving honor to the Jewish inheritance of Pharisaic Christians by attributing to the Mosaic institution a most significant place in God's scheme of things for the Jewish people, and certainly any and all Jewish Christians in Jerusalem, including those whom he called false brothers who came in to spy out his freedom in Jesus Messiah, and with whom he soon found himself in conflict (Gal. 2:4), could take no offense at this. All would have been well between Paul and the Pharisaic Christians had Paul stopped here.

But Paul went further. He superscribed a second covenant from God, through Jesus, which covenant was the superior revelation and which covenant is to serve the purpose ultimately of superseding the Mosaic covenant. And the Pharisaic Christians did take offense. They were convinced that Paul was destroying the primary significance of God's covenant through Moses.

Furthermore the older Christians in Jerusalem took offense at Paul. Not only did they regard Paul's two covenant theory as a forthright denial of the singularity and eternity of God's word. They thought Paul was minimizing the Christian covenant by allowing for the Mosaic covenant.

Paul found himself not only in conflict with these Pharisaic Christians in Jerusalem. He found himself in conflict with James, Peter, John and Barnabas. Paul was disconcerted by the Jewish Christian disposition to one covenant, indeed a denial of their sacred inheritance from Judaism through Moses. Barnabas on the other hand, planning to work with Paul, accepted the singular covenant in stride because he had been exposed to this kind of attitude rather intimately during several years of close association with the Jerusalem Christians. Barnabas was quite concerned, however, as were the Jerusalem pillars, over Paul's doctrine of two covenants.

The Jerusalem community was compelled to insist on the singularity of God's covenant, which was based on their concept of God's nature and of God's word. God is eternal and his word in unchanging. His covenant is a reflection of his nature and of his word, which means that his covenant likewise is eternal and unchanging. It has to be singular. Any covenant which God gave through Abraham must of necessity be identical therefore with any subsequent revelation through Moses, all the prophets, and through Jesus. The changelessness of God's nature and the eternity of his word rise up to demand that his covenant is one and only one. It could be no other way, and God's covenant is the sole possession of all those throughout the ages who understand God's singular and consistent revelation through his prophets, whether God spoke through Abraham, Isaac, Jacob, Moses, Joshua, David, Jeremiah, Ezekiel, Daniel, Enoch or anyone else and finally through Jesus. In all cases God's message is the same. The Jerusalem church insisted that the covenant through Abraham God revealed repeatedly throughout the ages through all the prophets until at last God clarified it through Jesus. It is unheard of and contrary to God's nature or intent that he would give a covenant, then supersede or abrogate it so that it forfeits its place for another.

Do we have any evidence in early Christian literature that the early Christians in Jerusalem were single covenanters? This single covenant attitude of the early Jerusalem Christians is in keeping with the purpose of Jesus who said, according to their understanding, "This is my blood of the covenant". Some texts insert new before covenant as in Mark 14:24 and Matthew 26:28, making the statement read, "This is my blood of the new covenant". This adjusted attitude allowing for two covenants would be normal after 70 A.D., after the Christian community of Jerusalem moved to Pella, then vanished into oblivion, and after the two covenant theory of Paul became normative in Christian thought because of a victorious gentile church and Paul's influence upon it.

How did the Jerusalem nucleus react to Paul's two covenant theory? Peter, James, John, Barnabas, the whole Jerusalem nucleus withstood Paul on his two covenant theory. Their Levitic inheritance and their Jerusalem environment demanded this of them. Unable to convince Paul of his error, and unable to accept Paul's unthinkable inconsistency (even though this inconsistency ultimately served to make Christianity congenial to the gentile world, something which they did not foresee), the Jerusalem group did not know what to do with him, and Barnabas soon realized that he had reached an impasse with Paul.

40

How did they regard Paul's doctrine of two covenants? As ridiculous and absurd! They were able to convince some Pharisaic Christians in Jerusalem that Jesus is the covenant of God, but Paul's two covenants spell an impossibility because they are a forthright denial of the changelessness of God's nature and of the eternity of God's word. Furthermore by giving the Mosaic covenant a legitimate place in God's scheme of revelation, and by adding to it a second covenant through Jesus, Paul is not appeasing the Jewish Christians who have a Pharisaic heritage nor is he solving any problems which they are imposing upon him and the church. He is on the contrary making matters worse, more complex and complicated for himself, because he is opening the door for an argument between Jewish people and Christians as to which is the greater of two covenants with the relative merits of Moses and Jesus standing in the forefront of the argument.

It was unthinkable to the apostles in Jerusalem, the pillars of the church, and the Christian community in Jerusalem at large, that God would give two covenants, each of them different indeed, one through Moses for Jewish people and another through Jesus for Christians, because God's law is singular, eternal and unchanging. God has dispensed only one covenant. God revealed his covenant to Moses, and Moses understood it. But the people did not receive it. While Moses was on the mountain they apostasized to the idolatry of molten images. Moses did not deliver God's covenant to them. He shattered it to pieces before they received it. This means that Judaism is not the product of God's covenant revealed to Moses, and Christianity has from Judaism absolutely no meaningful religious inheritance. The authenticity of Christianity reaches back to Abraham. With this separation from the Judaic institution fully accomplished the Jerusalem colleagues closed completely and forever the door to any right which Pharisaic Christians might think they have to judaize gentile Christians or to teach them about the priority of Mosaic law.

In spite of apparent differences Paul reports that the pillars Peter, James and John gave to him and Barnabas the right hand of fellowship, that they should be partners in preaching the gospel of Messiah to the gentiles. They expected Paul and Barnabas to work together as a team. We wish that we had an account of this occasion written by Peter or by James or by John. We suspect that it would have a somewhat different flavor. The Jerusalem pillars thought that Barnabas would be a very good influence on Paul, certainly able to bring Paul to a better understanding of the Christian covenant. They laid upon Paul and Barnabas only one stipulation, namely, that they should remember the poor (Gal. 2:9-10). Paul and Barnabas returned together with Titus to Antioch.

How will Paul and Barnabas honor this stipulation? They will take collections from their churches, carry the proceeds to Jerusalem and give the money for the use of the poor Christians. In that he established his churches in Syria and Cilicia before the pillars charged him to remember the poor Paul was under no obligation to take collections from those churches.

The author of The Acts of the Apostles tells an entirely different story about Paul and Barnabas, placing them together on two trips from Antioch to Jerusalem as we have already noticed: (1) they delivered charitable relief from the Antioch church to the Jerusalem Christians (Acts 11:27-30), and (2) they attended together the Jerusalem Council (Acts 15:1-35).

After Barnabas went to Tarsus and located Paul they went together to Antioch; and soon thereafter, approximately one year, prophets from Jerusalem appeared in Antioch. One of them, Agabus, prophesied a famine over all the world, whereupon the Antioch brothers decided to send charitable relief to the Judean brothers, which gifts Paul and Barnabas delivered to the Jerusalem elders.

Teachers from Judea some time later appeared in Antioch insisting that salvation is contingent upon all converts including gentiles submitting to circumcision. Christians indeed comprise the true Israel, are indeed children of Abraham, and children of Abraham must authenticate this allegiance by the rite of circumcision. These judaizers generated a disturbance in the Antioch church which caused no small concern; Paul and Barnabas, recently returned from their first missionary journey, soon found themselves engaged against them in lively dispute. But this was not enough. They must settle this problem in a most authoritative and conclusive manner. The Antioch church appointed Paul and Barnabas along with others to journey to Jerusalem and consult the apostles and elders about this matter.

They arrived in Jerusalem only to find that some of the believers within the Pharisaic bloc of the Jerusalem church insisted that gentiles be circumcised and required to adhere to the law of Moses. But the apostles and elders in Jerusalem refused to submit to the demands of these Pharisaic Christians. They assembled to consider the problem. Peter delivered a brief address relating how God visited the gentiles to call them to be his people, stressing the priority of faith and salvation through grace as quite adequate for gentiles. Barnabas and Paul related what God through them had accomplished among the gentiles. James climaxed the meeting with a speech in which he supported the recommendations of Peter. The assembly concluded that a letter to the gentiles was in order, not only to the gentiles of Antioch but also to those throughout Syria and Cilicia recommending that they shall abstain from the pollutions of idols, from unchastity, from what is strangled and from blood. But they found no reason to give Moses, in that he has been preached in every city for many generations and is read in the synagogues every sabbath, any further impetus by imposing the law of Moses on gentile converts to Christianity.

The Jerusalem community after composing the letter selected two of their leaders, Judas and Silas, to accompany Barnabas and Paul on their return to Antioch and to report personally the Jerusalem decision to the Antioch church as well as to deliver the letter. After fulfilling their assignment Judas and Silas returned to Jerusalem. Paul and Barnabas remained in Antioch.

42

This assembly in Jerusalem to consider the problem of circumcision is that occasion which is usually referred to as the Jerusalem Council.

It is strange indeed that this council, though it met to legislate on the problem of circumcision, concluded not a single recommendation and passed absolutely no legislation concerning circumcision. Instead the council deliberated on pollutions of idols, unchastity, things strangled and blood. The author of The Acts, as is apparent from his account of the Jerusalem Council, tied together Paul and Barnabas, Peter and James with a singularity of purpose and harmony of action, all of which is in reality a very superficial representation. Nevertheless The Acts has Barnabas, Peter and James lending dramatic support to the Pauline priority of faith and salvation through grace. The author is at the same time quite aware of the leading position which James held in the Jerusalem community. It was the judgment of James lending support to Pauline attitudes which determined the action of the council.

These two trips which the author of The Acts reports that Paul and Barnabas made from Antioch to Jerusalem, and back to Antioch, (1) to deliver charitable relief to the Jerusalem Christians, and (2) to attend the Jerusalem Council, offers difficulties. Why? Because Paul reports only one trip to Jerusalem with Barnabas, and his purpose is entirely different: to explain to the pillars the gospel which he was preaching to the gentiles in Syria and Cilicia (Gal. 2:2). This situation raises two questions: (1) Did Paul and Barnabas make together a journey from Antioch to Jerusalem to deliver famine relief as The Acts reports? (2) Did Paul and Barnabas make together a journey from Antioch to Jerusalem to attend the Jerusalem Council as The Acts reports? It would seem that had Paul and Barnabas made these two trips together from Antioch to Jerusalem they would have been of such vital importance in the life of the Antioch and Jerusalem churches, as well as to the agenda of Paul himself, that somewhere Paul would have mentioned them, the same as he mentioned his trip with Barnabas and Titus to explain to the pillars the gospel which he was preaching to the gentiles. But nowhere did Paul mention either of these two eventful trips. And since Paul did not mention them we now face two problems: (1) Can we equate this first journey which The Acts 11:27-30 reports that Paul and Barnabas made, that of taking famine relief from Antioch to Jerusalem, with the trip which Paul actually made to Jerusalem with Barnabas and Titus (Gal. 2:2)? (2) Can we equate this second journey which The Acts 15:1-35 reports that Paul and Barnabas made, that of attending the Jerusalem Council, with the trip which Paul actually made to Jerusalem with Barnabas and Titus (Gal. 2:2)?

(1) Paul is unaware that he and Barnabas on their trip together from Antioch to Jerusalem delivered famine relief to Jerusalem. He makes not the slightest mention of it. The Jerusalem pillars charged them, Barnabas and Paul, to remember the poor (Gal. 2:10) that is, they are to receive collections from the churches which they will be establishing among the gentiles to contribute to the welfare of the Jerusalem Christians who are poor. If Paul had already performed such a charitable mission from Antioch the pillars would have commended him

43

for it. Or certainly Paul would have reminded them that he was already aware of this obligation! Or more ironic still it would have been quite unnecessary for them to remind Paul to be sure to fulfill an obligation of which he had already demonstrated his full awareness! And if Paul had actually exercised such beneficence toward the Jerusalem Christians it would have given Paul a precedent, a bit of added punch, which he could have used to encourage this charity in the churches which he later established in Philippi, Thessalonica, Corinth, Galatia and possibly Ephesus, namely, to make collections for the Jerusalem poor. But the only precedent which he had with these churches was the request by the pillars when he visited them in Jerusalem. From Paul's account of his own activities which he relates to the Galatians we are unable to support a trip which The Acts reports that Paul and Barnabas made from Antioch to Jerusalem to carry famine relief to Jerusalem.

(2) Can we equate The Acts 15:1-35 trip to attend the Jerusalem Council, the second trip which The Acts reports of Paul and Barnabas from Antioch to Jerusalem, with the actual trip which Paul, Barnabas and Titus made together from Antioch to Jerusalem (Gal. 2:2)? Both Galatians and The Acts contain a singular detail which encourages the suspicion that they are reporting a single occasion. What is this singular detail? The problem of circumcision. Even though some of the brothers, whom Paul calls false brothers, demanded that Titus who was a Greek be circumcised, they refused to submit to their demands; and this detail about Titus was unknown to the author of The Acts. Paul identified James as the leader of the circumcision party (Gal. 2:12), another detail of which the author of The Acts is apparently unaware. At the actual meeting in Jerusalem with the pillars, Paul reports, James along with Peter and John gave approval that Paul and Barnabas should carry the gospel to the gentiles, that is, the uncircumcised (Gal. 2:7-9). Paul regarded this gesture certainly as an agreement that circumcision of gentiles is quite unnecessary for their salvation, and Titus remained uncircumcised.

Paul is unaware that he traveled with Barnabas from Antioch to Jerusalem to attend a Jerusalem Council. He makes no mention of such a trip for this purpose. In his argument against circumcision with the Galatians he was unable to quote a decree by the Jerusalem Council, which would have been an impregnable apostolic dictum on circumcision. His only recourse was a recollection that when he and Barnabas met with the pillars in Jerusalem Titus was not compelled to be circumcised, his evidence that this rite is superflous for gentile converts. And further if Paul actually attended a council in Jerusalem which deliberated on the problems of food sacrificed to idols, blood, things strangled and unchastity, it seems strange that he did not quote the decree of this council to the Corinthians (I Cor. 8:1, 4, 7, 10, 10:19, 28) in his lengthy discussion with them about meats offered to idols, and to the Romans (Rom. 14:2-3, 6, 20) in his discussion of food questions with them! A decree from the Jerusalem apostles would have been definitive and beyond dispute. His appeal to such a decree would have been far more effective, certainly far more convincing, than all those other arguments which Paul was able to muster! Yet Paul remained silent on the council.

Following such a council Peter's conduct in Antioch when he visited there and ate with gentiles, then withdrew from them, would have been most surprising! It would also be as greatly surprising if Peter actually had a vision as recorded in The Acts 10:1-43. Paul in his rebuke of Peter would have reminded Peter doubtlessly of the decisions of the council as well as of his vision of foods clean and unclean.

The fact now stands that Paul and Barnabas made one trip together to Jerusalem. They did not make two trips as the author of The Acts reports. Did Paul and Barnabas carry charitable relief from the Antioch church to the Jerusalem church? To this question we must conclude: No! Did Paul with Barnabas attend a Jerusalem Council? To this question we must conclude: No! Can the trip which Paul reported in his letter to the Galatians, from Antioch to Jerusalem with Barnabas and Titus, to discuss with the pillars of the Jerusalem church the gospel which he was preaching among the gentiles, be correlated to either of these two trips reported in The Acts? To this we must reply: No!

But if Paul and Barnabas made only one trip together to Jerusalem, what process evolved the accounts recorded by the author of The Acts? How can we account for the fact that The Acts reports two different trips, neither of which correlates to the actual trip which Paul and Barnabas made? Two cities are involved, Jerusalem and Antioch. Jerusalem was the center of apostolic Christianity. When Paul made his first trip to Jerusalem three years after the risen Jesus appeared in him he proposed to identify with the Jerusalem nucleus as an equivalent with James and Peter. His credentials were just as good as were the credentials of James. They rejected him, whereupon Paul went to Syria and Cilicia and became quite influential in the Antioch church. Antioch fast came to the front as the leading center for gentile Christianity. And Paul was preaching a rather strange Christian message. The apostles in Jerusalem felt obligated to direct, even control the Christian movement not only in Jerusalem but also in the gentile world. How can the Jerusalem church remedy this situation and exercise control over one whom they had earlier rejected? Only by confronting him in Jerusalem, and Barnabas became the instrument to accompany Paul to such a meeting.

Would not each of these cities, both Antioch and Jerusalem, have its own story about the trip which Paul and Barnabas made together to Jerusalem!

What would be the Jerusalem version of the trip? Barnabas, who had worked with the apostles in Jerusalem for several years and who had since turned his attention to the gentile mission, whereupon he would have something in common with Paul, invited Paul to come to Jerusalem and discuss with the pillars problems which Paul had generated on the gentile arena in Syria and Cilicia. Paul accepted the invitation, accomplished the journey, the Jerusalem leaders listened to him, then tried to get him to understand better God's covenant revealed to his people through his prophets and at last through Jesus so that Paul could perform more effectively his mission to the gentiles. Paul came to Jerusalem, so the Jerusalem nucleus would insist, to receive

45

instructions from the pillars, whereupon after they reached agreement they gave Paul their approval. An echo of this attitude is later mixed in with The Acts account of the Jerusalem Council.

Antioch as the center for Gentile Christianity is fast stealing the pennant from Jerusalem and rivalry between these two leading Christian centers had long since begun to brew. Would not Antioch have its version likewise of the story of Paul's visit to Jerusalem? Paul went to Jerusalem to carry gifts from Antioch to Jerusalem to relieve the poverty of the Jerusalem brothers, a very generous expression of kindness and concern by the Antioch brothers. Paul went not to consult the pillars of the church, not to justify his preaching, not to get their approval, but rather he went to Jerusalem to perform an act of charity.

So we hypothesize that the author of The Acts fell heir to two different traditions about the journey of Paul and Barnabas to Jerusalem, the Jerusalem tradition and the Antioch tradition. But he did not recognize them as modified accounts of a single occasion. These two traditions were so different that the author of The Acts thought them to be two different accounts of two entirely different journeys, so he treated them as such: one to take famine relief from Antioch (Acts 11:27-30, 12:15), and the other to attend the Jerusalem Council (Acts 15:1-35). By the time the Jerusalem version reached the ears of the author of The Acts it had become somewhat changed. He knew of Paul's problems over circumcision on the gentile arena as well as in Jerusalem. Also he was aware of a council which met in Jerusalem to legislate on circumcision. He judged though erroneously when he put these two things together that Barnabas and Paul went to Jerusalem to attend the Jerusalem Council.

How can we account for the discrepancy of this council, meeting to deliberate on circumcision, concluding nothing on circumcision whatever, but passing legislation on entirely different matters? This very strange situation reported by The Acts leads us to judge that there were in reality two different councils in Jerusalem which deliberated on two entirely different problems. The author of The Acts had inadequate information and he condensed them into a single council. His information about Paul was inaccurate, and he made his condensed single Jerusalem Council the object of Paul's visit to Jerusalem.

Paul and Barnabas made neither of these two trips together to Jerusalem which The Acts reports. Likewise Paul and Barnabas attended neither of the two Jerusalem councils. These councils met after Paul and Barnabas visited with the pillars in Jerusalem, and Paul, if he knew of these two councils, would not feel bound by their decisions because he had already received personal approval from the pillars. The author of The Acts is thoroughly misinformed about the movements of Paul and Barnabas.

But Paul and Barnabas did travel together to Jerusalem! They made only one such trip together, and this trip was for none of the purposes related by the author of The Acts. They went to Jerusalem together, as Paul states, to lay before the pillars of the church the gospel which

46

he preached to the gentiles. In the routine of the visit they disputed over circumcision. And Paul got what he interpreted to be apostolic approval from the Jerusalem pillars for his mission to the gentiles.

Soon after Paul, Barnabas and Titus returned to Antioch Peter came to Antioch to visit them. Probably much more was involved than a friendly and personal visit. Why did Peter come to Antioch? This would give him certainly ample opportunity to get acquainted with the gentile church in Antioch, but more probably such a visit was arranged before Paul and Barnabas left Jerusalem to return to Antioch, so that Peter could help them plan their offensive into the gentile world. In the routine of his visit Peter enjoyed himself and dined with gentiles such as to ignore the stipulations of his Jewish inheritance. James was the leader of the circumcision party in the Jerusalem church, and he sent emissaries to Antioch to check up and see that matters progressed in a manner compatible with his interests. Upon the appearance in Antioch of emissaries from James, Peter who wanted no static from James and his circumcision party withdrew along with other Jewish Christians from eating with gentiles. In view of his association with Peter and the Jerusalem church for several years it was natural for Barnabas to go in Peter's direction, merely an automatic reaffirmation of his inheritance and of his sympathies with the Jerusalem outlook. But Paul regarded this as duplicity on the part of Peter. He resented Peter's duplicity. He already has the approval of the pillars, including Peter, from his Jerusalem visit. They cannot take this away from him. He need not contain himself in his reaction. He spoke out rather boldly rebuking Peter for his vacillation. The whole situation served to convince Paul that an indefinite association with Barnabas would be certainly impossible.

Paul writes with possibly a degree of regret, "even Barnabas was carried away by their insincerity" (Gal. 2:13), reflecting that his plans to team with Barnabas never matured. He understood fairly well all the time that any partnership with Barnabas could be at the best only precarious and at the most only temporary, because their disagreement was apparent. There was no way for Paul to overcome his differences with Barnabas and the Jerusalem Christians. Had these emissaries from James stayed home in Jerusalem the plans for Paul and Barnabas to team together probably would have matured. But the Antioch occasion served to make unnecessary what would have been a very bitter confrontation at a later date.

Paul is unaware that he had made earlier a missionary journey with Barnabas through Cyprus, Pamphylia, Pisidia and Lycaonia (Acts 13:4-14:26).

What was Paul's itinerary after his Antioch quarrel with Peter? He parted company with Barnabas, which was in reality only a failure to team with Barnabas, in 44 A.D., and planned to turn his attention to Macedonia and Achaia. Did his churches in Syria and Cilicia know of his trip to Jerusalem? Were they anxious to learn the outcome of the trip? Would it be most unusual after eleven years with them, hardly compatible with his character, for Paul to disappear suddenly into

47

Europe without explaining to them the outcome of his trip with Barnabas and Titus to Jerusalem, and without saying farewell to them? Before he left Antioch to go to Macedonia did Paul revisit his churches in Syria and Cilicia? We judge that this would be Paul's foremost concern before leaving the area. Certainly he would want his churches to know that he had received the approval of the Jerusalem nucleus to preach the gospel of Messiah to the gentile world, and to receive their good wishes as he turned his attention to a new arena anxious to demonstrate that he is worthy of the good faith which the pillars have placed in him. We do not know how many churches Paul had in Syria and Cilicia. We do not know the cities where they were located. We do not know how long it would have taken him to revisit them. We do know however that Syria and Cilicia were fairly extensive in size, and in eleven years he could have established there a fair number of churches. Approximately one year of time required for revisiting these churches is a reasonable guess, which would carry him well into 45 A.D.

Perhaps an echo of Paul's revisiting his churches in Syria and Cilicia is reflected in The Acts 15:41: "And he went through Syria and Cilicia strengthening the churches".

How did Paul get to Philippi? He might have traveled over land, in a hurry, minimizing his missionary activities while crossing Asia Minor, anxious to begin his work in the Greek world of Macedonia. More probably, after revisiting his Christian friends throughout Syria and Cilicia, he returned to Antioch, then traveled to Europe by means of boat.

Why do we judge in favor of Paul's trip to Europe by way of the sea? Just after he returned to Ephesus from his quick and painful visit to Corinth, in his third and severe letter to the Corinthians 54 A.D. Paul listed the misfortunates which befell him, as we have already noticed, throughout the years in the routine of his preaching the gospel. Paul declares that he was shipwrecked three times and that he was adrift at sea for a day and a night (II Cor. 11:25), events which had to occur prior to 54 A.D. when he wrote of them.

When and on what journey before 54 A.D. was Paul shipwrecked? When and on what journey before 54 A.D. was Paul adrift at sea for a day and a night?

What trips did Paul make by boat? We judge that Paul, after one and one-half years in Corinth, traveled by boat from Corinth to Ephesus in 51 A.D. Is it reasonable for us to assume that if Paul had been shipwrecked on this trip he would have mentioned the occasion to the Corinthians in one of the four letters which he later wrote to them? We think so. And yet, even though Paul declares to the Corinthians in his third letter that he was shipwrecked three times, he never relates shipwreck to this trip across the Aegean sea from Corinth to Ephesus. Why? Because no shipwreck occurred on this trip.

The Acts reports that Paul met Aquila and Prisca in Corinth (18:2) and that Aquila and Prisca sailed with Paul from Corinth to Ephesus (18:18). If Paul had been shipwrecked on the Aegean sea with Aquila and Prisca during this trip from Corinth to Ephesus, is it reasonable to assume that Paul would have mentioned it later when writing his second letter to the Corinthians in which he sent greetings from Aquila and Prisca (I Cor. 16:19)? Would not such an event have been on his mind with his mention of Aquila and Prisca, and would he not have mentioned it? We think that he would have.

Paul no doubt traveled by boat on his quick and painful visit to Corinth from Ephesus, then back to Ephesus in 54 A.D. at which point he sat down immediately, wasting no time, and wrote his third and severe letter to Corinth. Was Paul shipwrecked on this trip? Certainly not! If he had been shipwrecked on this quick and painful visit to Corinth which would only have added deeper injury to his already unbearable misery over the Corinthian situation would he have mentioned it? Is it reasonable to assume that he would have made specific reference to it? Would it still have been in the forefront of his mind immediately on his return to Ephesus? We think so. And if he had been shipwrecked on this trip, either in route to Corinth or in return to Ephesus, and failed to mention it in his letter, he then let pass by certainly a golden opportunity to tie this misfortune into an immediate relationship with his Corinthian frustrations.

During the earlier half of Paul's stay in Ephesus he probably went up into Galatia and established his churches there. How did he travel? Did he go by land or did he go by way of the sea? He could have gone by boat from Ephesus to Troas, then inland to Galatia, and on leaving Galatia he could have traveled to Troas and returned from Troas to Ephesus by way of the sea. We know later that Paul was acquainted with the Christians in Troas (II Cor. 2:12). Would Paul have been shipwrecked on a trip such as this? We have no reason to think so.

When was Paul shipwrecked three times? When was he adrift at sea for a day and a night? He writes of these misfortunes along with other sufferings and various maltreatments as if they occurred to him in a more distant past. We judge in favor of Paul's trip from Antioch of Syria to Philippi in Macedonia by way of the sea because this is the only time we can identify when such casualties at sea could have occurred to him. In any case a trip from Antioch to Philippi would require a few months, to bring Paul into the very early months of 46 A.D. upon his arrival in Europe.

The author of The Acts (17:14) has Paul traveling from Beroea to Athens probably by way of the sea, but makes no mention of shipwreck.

What was Paul's first European stop? Paul's first European stop was Philippi in Macedonia where he worked approximately two years, early 46 A.D. into 48 A.D., establishing a church in Philippi. Paul

was treated shamefully in Philippi, and the Thessalonians in addition
to the Philippians were aware of this (I Thes. 2:2). We do not know
exactly what this shameful treatment in Philippi was. Paul does not
specify. It included imprisonment. It still lingered on in his mind,
perhaps haunted him, two years later, 50 A.D., when he wrote to the
Thessalonians from Corinth. And in early 54 A.D. writing from Ephesus
to the Philippians Paul recalls that while he was in Thessalonica the
Christians in Philippi sent financial assistance to him twice (Phil.
4:16), while he was in Corinth they sent aid to him once (II Cor. 11:9),
and while imprisoned in Ephesus they sent further assistance (Phil.
4:18), which means that Paul was in Philippi long enough to establish
excellent rapport with a very satisfactory community of Christian
believers, his only church from which he was willing to accept funds
for his personal use (Phil. 4:15).

The author of The Acts (16:23-24), aware that Paul was shamefully
treated in Philippi, fills in the missing parts by having Paul and Silas
in Philippi beaten with rods and imprisoned in the inner part of the
prison with their feet in the stocks. He allows Paul possibly two weeks
in Philippi (16:13) but Paul's letters reveal that his achievements
there would have required much more time than two weeks.

After nourishing the church in Philippi to the point where he was
willing to leave it where did Paul go? From Philippi Paul moved west
to Thessalonica and proceeded to build a community of Christian believers
there, an accomplishment which likewise as in Philippi would have
required about two years, early 48 A.D. into late 49 A.D. or early 50
A.D. During his stay in Thessalonica Paul worked day and night to earn
his own subsistence, so that he would be in no way a financial burden
to the Thessalonians (I Thes. 2:9), during which time also the Philippians twice sent gifts to him (Phil. 4:16). Paul had to be in Thessalonica, not only long enough to establish a church to the point where
it could carry itself, but also long enough to establish himself as a
tradesman, and long enough for the Philippian Christians to send gifts
to him on two occasions. How long would it have taken him to establish
himself as a tradesman? What were the occasions of the Philippians
sending these gifts? Very possibly it would have required a year or
more for him to become effective in a new environment at a trade, and
the gifts might well have been anniversary memorials, expressions of
gratitude by the Philippians on the anniversaries of Paul's first
appearance in Philippi.

The author of The Acts (17:2) allows Paul possibly three weeks in
Thessalonica, but his letters reveal that his achievements in Thessalonica would have required more than three weeks.

With the church established adequately in Thessalonica, what was
Paul's next move? Accompanied by Silas and Timothy, Paul moved south
to Athens. It seems that as soon as Paul left Thessalonica his enemies

were determined to discredit him (I Thes. 2:3). Paul sent Timothy from
Athens back to Thessalonica to try to correct the difficulties (I Thes.
3:1-2). Meanwhile Paul and Silas went on to Corinth where Timothy
later rejoined them and reported on the Thessalonian situation (I Thes.
3:6).

The author of The Acts (17:5, 10-15, 18:1) tells quite a different
story. Because of an uproar in Thessalonica caused by jealous Jewish
people the brothers sent Paul and Silas by night to Beroea where Paul
pursued his preaching activities; but Jewish people from Thessalonica
followed Paul to Beroea to cause further trouble, whereupon the brothers
sent Paul by way of the sea to Athens. Silas and Timothy remained in
Beroea, until they received word to rejoin Paul in Athens as soon as
possible. Paul, Silas and Timothy then left Athens together and moved
on to Corinth.

Timothy probably carried a letter from the Thessalonians to Paul,
and this letter along with Timothy's report prompted Paul to write to
the Thessalonians immediately on Timothy's arrival, his very first
letter to any of his Christian communities. Paul expressed his hope
that he would return to them soon (I Thes. 3:10-11). This hope did not
mature. Paul soon became involved in Corinth and throughout the region
of Achaia, not limiting his activities to the city of Corinth alone
(I Cor. 1:2, II Cor. 1:1). After a year and a half, from early 50 A.D.
until well into 51 A.D., his interests turned him instead to go to
Ephesus.

It is noteworthy that the author of The Acts (18:11) has fairly
reliable information about the length of time Paul stayed in Corinth:
"a year and six months".

Ephesus was the crossroads of the Christian world; it became a
great Christian center, greater than Antioch, greater than Jerusalem.
Sooner or later itinerant Christian workers from the whole Mediterranean
world filtrated into Ephesus. This city offered Paul a broad scope of
associations. Paul made Ephesus his headquarters, his base of opera-
tions, for the next three and one-half years, from middle 51 A.D. until
late 54 A.D. What comprised Paul's activities during this three and
one-half years in Ephesus? He kept in close touch with his churches
by means of messengers, some of them itinerant workers in the churches,
others messengers from his churches who sought his advice on various
kinds of problems, in some cases by personal visits which Paul himself
made and in other cases by visits which his messengers Titus and
Timothy made to his churches; Paul wrote most of his letters to his
churches, all of them except three, from Ephesus during this time; he
was in touch with other churches, churches which he did not establish,
in western Asia Minor; and he probably established his own church in
Ephesus.

51

When did Paul establish his churches in Galatia? His letter to
them reflects a disposition of immediacy. They are still in their
infancy: "I am astonished that you are so soon deserting him who called
you in the grace of Messiah. . ." (Gal. 1:6). It took only a brief
interim of Paul's absence for trouble to brew in Thessalonica, and then
in Corinth, approximately one year for it to reach distressing proportions in Corinth, and we can judge that it would have required nearly
the same amount of time for the bubble to burst in Galatia.

There is a remote possibility that Paul, after his quarrel with
Peter in Antioch, did not revisit his churches in Syria and Cilicia,
but instead traveled overland through Asia Minor to Galatia, established
his Galatian churches, and then moved on to Philippi.

This suggestion only adds to our difficulties. If such were the
case Paul would have been removed from the Galatians by approximately
ten years when he wrote to them; it would have been somewhat unusual
for him not to have mentioned these churches to the Philippians and the
Thessalonians, and he could have done a much better job, since he would
have had behind him the experience of establishing the Galatian churches,
avoiding misunderstandings which his preaching generated among the
Thessalonians and the Corinthians; and the time element would have made
Paul's psychological disposition toward the Galatians somewhat different in his letter.

Such a suggestion also eliminates Paul's trip from Antioch of Syria
to Philippi of Macedonia by way of the sea, and this would in turn
eliminate the only occasion which we can judge appropriate for Paul's
being shipwrecked.

Paul probably traveled into the region of Galatia and established
his Galatian churches sometime during the earlier part of his three and
one-half years with headquarters in Ephesus. This is the only time in
his itinerary when we can account for his establishment of these churches.
He was unable to stay with the Galatians as long as he had stayed with
his other infant churches in Philippi, Thessalonica and Corinth. His
short stay with them only served to add fuel to their problems after he
left. They misunderstood his message.

Soon after Paul returned to Ephesus from Galatia he learned of a
most distressing situation among the Christians at Corinth. Who
delivered this message to Paul? We do not know. He was quite possibly
informed by an itinerant worker who had been in Corinth. The Corinthian church might have tried previously to contact Paul in Ephesus
only to learn that he was not available, and possibly even unknown and
unlocateable, because Paul had been in Ephesus a relatively short time,
only a few months, before going into Galatia. Upon receiving the message on the Corinthian situation Paul wrote a letter to Corinth, which
was probably the very first letter which he wrote from Ephesus,
instructing the Corinthian Christians to have no company with those
brothers within the church who persist in immorality. This letter is
now lost, except possibly for a very brief excerpt from it preserved
in II Corinthians 6:14-7:1.

During his interim in Ephesus, three and one-half years, Paul was in prison for a brief period, during which imprisonment he wrote Philippians, Philemon, Colossians and Ephesians. Some critics question the authenticity of Philemon, Colossians and Ephesians.

Paul was in close touch with the Philippian church. Before he wrote his letter to them two round trips from Ephesus to Philippi were made by unidentified messengers: (1) information about Paul's imprisonment reached Philippi, and the Philippian church sent Epaphroditus to stay with him as well as to carry some gifts to him (Phil. 4:18); (2) news of Epaphroditus' illness reached Philippi, and Paul learned of their concern for him (Phil. 2:26). After Epaphroditus recovered from his illness Paul sent him back to Philippi, and Epaphroditus carried with him Paul's letter to the Philippians (Phil. 2:25). It is clear from his letter that Paul is in prison; he mentions his bonds (Phil. 1:7, 12-14), but he does not mention the reason for imprisonment. Paul expects to send Timothy to them soon and then Paul expects to visit them himself (Phil. 2:19, 24). His anticipated visit is for the purpose of receiving collections for the Jerusalem brothers. He still remembers the gifts which the Philippians sent him while he was in Thessalonica and Corinth (Phil. 4:15-16, II Cor. 11:9).

Sometime in Ephesus Paul met Philemon whom Paul influenced to become a Christian. Philemon lived in Colossae, a town which is about one-hundred miles east of Ephesus. Paul later also in Ephesus, in prison, met Onesimus who was Philemon's runaway servant, whom he likewise converted to Christianity. Paul sent Onesimus back to Philemon accompanied by Tychicus along with a personal letter, Paul's only personal letter which has survived, which Tychicus delivered to Philemon.

Paul at the same time wrote to the Colossian Christians, which letter Tychicus also delivered. He wrote this letter with the approval of Epaphras who founded the church in Colossae, and who requested Paul's assistance regarding problems which had developed. He added a personal touch by expressing his hope that he would be able to visit them (Philm. 22, Col. 2:1).

Paul sent by Tychicus on the same trip a letter to the Laodiceans, a circular letter possibly intended for the Christians of the Lycus river valley, churches not founded by Paul but founded probably by Epaphras who worked there as well as in Colossae (Col. 1:8, 4:12-13). This letter now bears the name Ephesians.

After the Corinthian Christians received Paul's first letter, in which he instructed them to separate from those who persist in immorality, some servants of Chloe who traveled from Corinth to Ephesus reported to Paul about the Corinthian situation. Soon thereafter the Corinthian church wrote a letter to Paul, a letter explaining the various disturbances within the church, requesting Paul's help. The church assigned the delivery of this letter to a delegation comprised of three of its members, Stephanus, Fortunatus and Achaicus who could also personally discuss the disturbances with Paul (I Cor. 16:17). Paul sent Timothy to Corinth to help alleviate the difficulties. After Timothy was on his way Paul wrote his second letter to the Corinthians, his response to the reports which he received from the servants of Chloe and from the three messengers Stephanus, Fortunatus and Achaicus, informing them that Timothy is in route and how they are to receive him (I Cor. 4:17, 16:10).

This is an unusual situation: Timothy leaves for Corinth, then Paul writes a letter to the Corinthians which he expects to reach Corinth before Timothy arrives. What reasonable explanation can we give for this? Paul was planning to send Timothy to Philippi (Phil. 2:19). Did he send Timothy first to Philippi, then to Corinth on one and the same trip? We judge that this is what he did, and that he sent his letter straight to Corinth across the Aegean sea probably carried by Stephanus, Fortunatus and Achaicus who would return to Corinth before Timothy arrived.

Timothy performed his assignment and returned to Paul in Ephesus with gloomy news from Corinth. He did not impress the Corinthians, who were disposed to think that they did not have to take instructions from him. Timothy was too weak a personality to overcome this stigma and solve their difficulties. Timothy's adverse report moved Paul to action. He traveled to Corinth himself, two-hundred-fifty miles across the sea, a quick and painful visit, to confront the troublemakers in Corinth and remedy the situation. The troublemakers were as adamant with Paul as they had been with Timothy, compelling him to defend himself against his inability to work miracles and against his not having an ecstatic gift.

At the pen of the author of The Acts of the Apostles Paul becomes a fantastic worker of miracles, with power to strike Bar-Jesus blind in such a way as to produce Christian faith in others (13:9-12), and with power to heal a man at Lystra who was lame from birth (14:8-10). At Philippi he cast a demon out of a soothsaying slave girl (16:16-18). In Ephesus Paul touched handkerchiefs and aprons which imbued these objects with power to heal diseases which infected the sick (19:12). At Troas he restored life to the young man Eutychus who fell out of the third story window (20:9-12). On the island of Malta Paul suffered no injury from a viper's bite (28:3), healed the father of Publius from fever and dysentery (28:8), then healed all the other people on the island from their diseases (28:9).

What does Paul tell about himself in this respect? He possessed the gift of speaking in tongues (I Cor. 14:18), but he was not a worker of miracles. He had to defend himself against the Corinthian brothers who belittled him because of his inability to work miracles (I Cor. 12:27-31). He did not have the gift of healing. Yet the author of The Acts has Paul working various kinds of miracles in Cyprus, Lystra, Philippi, Ephesus, Troas and Malta in the routine of three missionary journeys and in route to Rome.

54

Paul returned from Corinth to Ephesus depressed, extremely disturbed, and dictated a blistering letter, his third to the Corinthians, part of which is now contained in II Corinthians 10-13.

As soon as Paul returned to Ephesus from his quick and painful trip to Corinth, his second visit there, he learned that the Galatian Christians had rather quickly deserted him to turn to a different gospel, and this situation evoked his letter to them. Paul probably wrote his third letter to the Corinthians at this very same time, a very severe letter to the Corinthians and another of the same general tone to the foolish Galatians. Paul names no city in Galatia, as if his letter is not addressed to a specific church, but it appears rather to be a circular letter which he is writing to several Christian communities in Galatia. Galatia was a Roman province in the northeast corner of what used to be Phrygia, two-hundred-fifty miles northeast of Ephesus, so named after Gauls who settled there in the third B.C. century and gained control of the trade route between east and west. Rome conquered the Gauls in 189 B.C. to make this area a buffer region between the east and the west, and formed in 25 B.C. the imperial Roman province of Galatia. This was the only area in Asia Minor bearing the name Galatia. These were the only people whom Paul could address as Galatians. We must expect this to be the area where Paul established his Galatian churches and to whom he sent his letter.

Paul wanted Titus to deliver his third letter, his severe letter to the Corinthians. Titus was reluctant. Timothy had failed in Corinth. Paul had failed in Corinth. What merit could he gain for himself, for Paul, for the Corinthian Christians by becoming a part of what he expected to be an additional failure? Paul finally persuaded him to accept the errand (II Cor. 8:16-24).

Meanwhile Paul must begin his program of visiting his churches to gather their collections for the Jerusalem Christians. He turned his attention first to Galatia, fast on the heels of his letter to them. While Paul is visiting his churches in Galatia Titus will carry his blistering letter to the Corinthians. They made plans to meet, after both errands were accomplished, in Troas or somewhere along a specified route in Macedonia.

Titus had not yet arrived in Troas when Paul got there, which did not alleviate Paul's disturbance over the Corinthians, so he excused himself from preaching to the Troas Christians to proceed to Macedonia. He met Titus somewhere in Macedonia. Titus brought good news to Paul about the situation in Corinth. Paul's quick and painful visit had been successful. The troublemakers have relented. Paul was so elated with Titus' report that immediately he wrote again to the Corinthians, his fourth letter to them, now partially preserved in II Corinthians 1:1-6:13, 7:2-9:15. Titus delivered this letter also.

Paul continued to visit his churches one by one throughout Macedonia and Achaia, gathering their collections for the Jerusalem poor, finally to arrive in Corinth.

How many trips did Paul make to Corinth? Paul reports three: (1) his first trip, 50 A.D., when he established the church, and his stay lasted approximately one and one-half years; (2) his second trip, 54 A.D., when he, after Timothy's failure, attempted to solve their numerous problems, a quick and painful visit from Ephesus to Corinth and back to Ephesus; (3) his third and final visit, 55 A.D., for the purpose of receiving their collections for the Jerusalem church, when he prolonged his stay with them, elated because, as a result of his second visit, they had set the church in proper order.

The author of The Acts is aware of only two trips which Paul made to Corinth: (1) his first appearance there, which lasted "a year and six months" (18:11), on his second missionary journey, and (2) his second trip there on his third missionary journey, with mention only of Greece, which we judge includes Corinth, which visit lasted three months (20:3).

We judge that Paul had more accurate information about his trips to Corinth than did the author of The Acts.

During his last visit to Corinth Paul wrote his last letter, known to us as his letter to the Romans.

His collections for the Jerusalem poor are now ready for delivery. After nine years of hard work Paul is ready at last to return to Jerusalem and in fulfillment of the stipulation placed upon him by the pillars of the church deliver the funds which he collected (Rom. 15: 25-28). After completing this errand Paul planned to visit the church in Rome and then go on to Spain.

After writing to the Romans and setting out for Jerusalem Paul disappeared from the scene. We do not know what happened to him. We have no information, no source of reliable information, and are therefore at a loss to know what happened to Paul. He probably never reached Jerusalem with his collections, nor did he get to Rome nor to Spain.

How many trips did Paul make to Jerusalem? Paul reports that he was in Jerusalem twice: (1) He went to Jerusalem and stayed with Peter for fourteen days, during which visit he met James but remained unknown by sight to the churches of Judea (Gal. 1:18-22). (2) He went to Jerusalem to discuss with the pillars of the Jerusalem church the gospel which he was preaching among the gentiles (Gal. 2:1-2). This was Paul's second trip to Jerusalem according to his own reports on his activities, and it is the last time he got to Jerusalem.

The author of The Acts takes Paul into Jerusalem on at least six different occasions: (1) from Tarsus of Cilicia, his home, to Jerusalem where he became a persecutor of Christians, (2) from Damascus, a return to Jerusalem after only a very brief stay in Damascus, (3) from

Antioch to Jerusalem with Barnabas to deliver charity for the Judean brothers to the elders in Jerusalem, (4) to attend the Jerusalem Council, from Antioch to Jerusalem, at the end of his first missionary journey, (5) to Jerusalem at the end of his second missionary journey, and (6) to Jerusalem at the end of his third missionary journey.

From the time the risen Jesus appeared in Paul in late 29 A.D. until his third and last visit to Corinth early 55 A.D. in preparation for his return to Jerusalem a quarter of a century, twenty-five years, passed by: three years in Arabia and Damascus, fifteen days with Peter in Jerusalem, eleven years in Syria and Cilicia, a brief trip from Antioch to Jerusalem with Barnabas and Titus and back to Antioch, possibly one year revisiting his churches in Syria and Cilicia, one-half year traveling to Macedonia, two years in Philippi, two years in Thessalonica, one and one-half years in Corinth, three and one-half years in Ephesus during which time he probably traveled into the Roman province of Galatia and established his churches there and returned to Ephesus, made his second trip to Corinth and returned to Ephesus, then revisited his churches in Galatia, Macedonia and Achaia to gather the collections for Jerusalem at the end of which he made his third and final visit to Corinth, activities which kept Paul fully occupied for a total of twenty-five years, allowing of course for a bit of travel time between places.

These activities in Arabia, Jerusalem, Syria and Cilicia, back to Jerusalem, back to Syria and Cilicia, across the sea to Philippi in Macedonia, on to Thessalonica, then to Athens and Corinth of Achaia, and western Asia Minor with headquarters in Ephesus, into Galatia, back to Ephesus, over to Corinth, back again to Ephesus, and a revisitation of all his churches in Galatia, Macedonia and Achaia kept Paul busy, in fact required all his time, from 29 A.D. into 55 A.D.

From the time Paul said farewell to Barnabas in Antioch 44 A.D., revisited his churches in Syria and Cilicia and sailed to Philippi, until at last Paul was ready to deliver the collections to Jerusalem 55 A.D., a total of eleven years, Paul for nine and possibly ten years remained on the soil of Macedonia, Achaia and Asia Minor, working to fulfill the request of the Jerusalem pillars.

Considering Paul from the viewpoint of what he tells us about himself in his letters we can divide his work on the Christian arena into three parts: (1) his three years in Damascus and Arabia, from late 29 A.D. until 32 A.D. or early 33 A.D., (2) his eleven years in Syria and Cilicia, from early 33 A.D. until 44 A.D., (3) his second trip to Jerusalem, with Barnabas and Titus, his return to Antioch, his quarrel with Peter, his separation from Barnabas, his probable revisitation of his churches and his trip from Antioch to Philippi, plus his nine or ten years in Macedonia, Achaia and western Asia Minor, from approximately 46 A.D. until 55 A.D. His trip to Jerusalem with Barnabas and Titus, when he received approval from the pillars for his work among the gentiles, marks a very significant turning point in his career.

It is appropriate for us to inquire at this point: Did Paul make three missionary journeys? We raise this question because the author of The Acts of the Apostles relates step by step and in eventful and picturesque detail the encounters of Paul and Barnabas as a missionary team sent out by the church of Antioch on a trip which took them through Cyprus, Pamphlyia, Pisidia, Lycaonia and the surrounding country, into the cities of Antioch, Iconium, Lystra and Derbe, that journey which is usually referred to as the first missionary journey, a trip which climaxed with a second visit together to Jerusalem.

Paul's first missionary journey (Acts, 13:4-14:26).

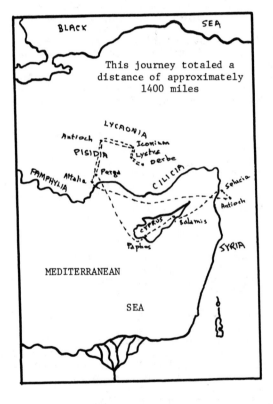

SYRIA
Antioch
Seleucia
CYPRUS
Salamis
Paphos
PAMPHYLIA
Perga
PISIDIA
Antioch
LYCAONIA
Iconium
Lystra
Derbe
Lystra
Iconium
PISIDIA
Antioch
PAMPHYLIA
Perga
Attalia
SYRIA
Antioch

What were Paul's experiences with Barnabas? Paul and Barnabas traveled together from Antioch to Jerusalem and back again to Antioch, accompanied by Titus. While in route to Jerusalem Barnabas discussed with Paul an arrangement whereby they would work together as a team in the gentile arena. In Jerusalem Paul got what he interpreted to be the approval of the pillars of the church to preach the gospel to the gentiles. After they returned to Antioch Peter visited them to help them plan their offensive together into the gentile world. Peter ate with gentiles. Emissaries from James arrived. Peter withdrew from gentile associations. Barnabas joined Peter in this duplicity. Paul used the occasion to dissolve his plans with Barnabas. They never accomplished any such journey together. The plans of Barnabas and Paul to work together never matured (Gal. 2:1-16).

The author of The Acts uses the first missionary journey as a turning point to get Barnabas off the stage and to place Paul on the center of the stage under the floodlights as gracefully as possible. Barnabas' presence assumes secondary significance during the journey, as if Barnabas is a kind of party of the second part. Even with the Jewish people, who are a source of perpetual trouble to Paul, Barnabas appears to have a different status. It is Paul who works miracles (the author of The Acts is unaware that Paul did not have this gift), does most of the preaching and who suffers stoning until he is believed to be dead.

Did Paul and Barnabas make such a missionary journey together? Paul is silent about such a journey. It would have been indeed a very extraordinary chapter in his experiences. But he seems to be unaware that he made such a journey. Furthermore, his very busy itinerary from late 29 A.D. until 55 A.D. which is reflected in his letters allows no time for such a journey.

This indicates further that John Mark did not desert them on a first journey, whereupon Barnabas and Paul had no occasion to argue over John Mark. The author of The Acts, not being well informed, used this argument as the occasion for Paul and Barnabas to separate from each other. He was unaware that Barnabas supported Peter's duplicity in Antioch. Paul in his letters gives not even a slightest suggestion about such an argument over John Mark.

Paul and Barnabas made only one trip together, a trip to Jerusalem when Paul got the approval of the pillars to preach the gospel to the gentiles, and back to Antioch. This is the only trip which they made together.

The author of The Acts goes on to describe step by step two more missionary journeys which Paul made with Silas and Timothy through Asia Minor, Macedonia and Achaia, each of these likewise ending with a visit to Jerusalem.

Paul's second missionary journey (Acts, 15:36-18:22).

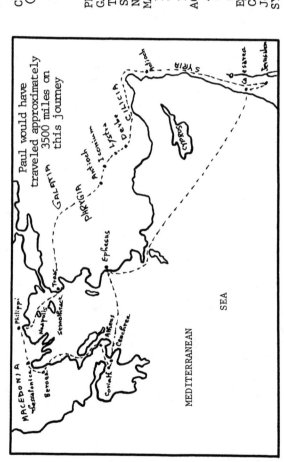

SYRIA
Antioch
CILICIA
(Lycaonia)
Derbe
Lystra
(Iconium)
(Antioch)
PHRYGIA
GALATIA
Troas
Samothrace
Neapolis
MACEDONIA
Philippi
Thessalonica
Beroea
ACHAIA
Athens
Corinth
Cenchrea
Ephesus
Caesarea
Jerusalem
SYRIA
Antioch

Paul's third missionary journey (Acts, 18:23-21:26).

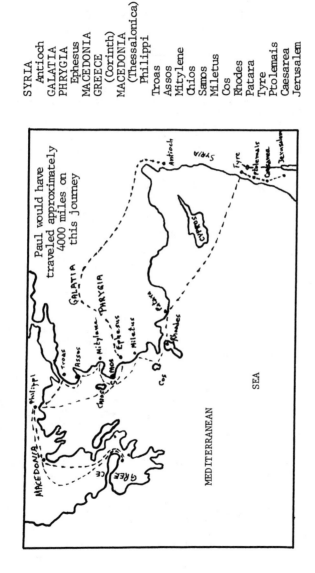

SYRIA
  Antioch
GALATIA
PHRYGIA
  Ephesus
MACEDONIA
GREECE
  (Corinth)
MACEDONIA
  (Thessalonica)
  Philippi
Troas
Assos
Mitylene
Chios
Samos
Miletus
Cos
Rhodes
Patara
Tyre
Ptolemais
Caesarea
Jerusalem

61

Did Paul make three missionary journeys? They would have been most important to him, to his missionary activities and to his relations with the Jerusalem and Antioch churches. Somewhere he certainly would have mentioned them. But he remains totally silent, and not even the slightest indication of three such journeys is reflected anywhere in his letters. He seems to be unaware that he made any such journeys.

We are unable to accept the three missionary journeys outline of Paul's activities in the gentile world.

After writing to the Roman Christians, informing them of his desire to preach the gospel in Rome and then move on to Spain, Paul was ready at last to travel to Jerusalem with the gifts from his churches. Did Paul write a letter to the Jerusalem Christians and tell them that he expected to see them in a few months? We think not. Were they expecting him after ten or eleven years of absence? They probably had no such expectation.

Did Paul set out from Corinth to Jerusalem by way of the sea? If so then he with his little band of delegates from his various churches-- Galatia, Philippi, Thessalonica, Corinth, possibly Ephesus--could have vanished and a year could pass by, possibly two years, before anyone would become aware that they were missing.

Was anyone anticipating a visit from Paul? Only the Romans. How much time will it take for the Romans to realize that Paul is not going to make it? One year? Two years?

Did Paul set out from Corinth to Jerusalem by way of land? The author of The Acts reports that Paul intended to sail from Corinth to Syria, but shifted his plans and went instead by land when he learned of a plot against him by some Jewish people (20:3).

Let us assume that Paul did suddenly change his plans and start for Jerusalem overland by way of Macedonia. Was anyone in Thessalonica expecting him? No. Was anyone in Philippi expecting him? No. Paul and his colleagues could have disappeared and no one would have become aware of it until much later.

Paul undoubtedly set out for Jerusalem but he and his colleagues never reached their destination.

The author of The Acts, interested in seeing that all of Paul's fondest hopes and dreams were fulfilled, especially his desire to preach the gospel in Rome, transports him back to Jerusalem where in the temple he was recognized, roundly abused by Jewish people, removed to Caesarea where he was imprisoned, and finally sent as a prisoner to Rome for trial (21:30-33, 23:23, 27:1).

We must judge that the author of The Acts, learning of Paul's several imprisonments as reported to the Corinthians (II Cor. 11:23), filled in the missing parts by fabricating his imprisonments in Caesarea and Rome. But he is short on chronology. Paul could not have been thinking of any possible imprisonments in Caesarea and in Rome when writing to the Corinthians because such could not yet have occurred.

Did Paul actually reach Jerusalem with the gifts from his churches? And was he in fact imprisoned in Caesarea and in Rome? We have no reliable evidence that Paul reached Jerusalem a third time. And we have located no Roman records of his imprisonments in Caesarea and in Rome. However, The Acts report is compensated by some equally fertile imaginations which report that Paul was martyred in Rome, beheaded by an executioner under Nero.

What happened to Paul? So far as we can determine he and the delegates from his churches disappeared soon after they left Corinth and we are inclined to judge that they never reached Jerusalem. They were probably robbed and killed soon after they left Corinth.

The esteem which the Christians developed for Paul by the turn of the century strongly suggests that he died a martyr's death.

PART III

PAUL'S LETTERS

I THESSALONIANS

When Paul wrote his letter to the Thessalonians, the very first letter he wrote which has survived, most of his work was done. He had been preaching the gospel since late 29 A.D., a total of twenty-one years. Only five years of his life remain.

Where had Paul been working before he arrived in Thessalonica? Philippi. Did he build a church in Philippi? He did. How was he treated there before moving on to Thessalonica? Shamefully (2:2).

How long did it take Paul to build the church in Thessalonica to the point where he was willing to leave it and move on? Paul does not make this as clear as we would like, but some of his casual comments give us a basis for hypothesis: (1) While in Thessalonica he worked day and night, presumably at his trade, so as not to be a financial burden to any of the Thessalonians (2:9). Paul does not identify his trade, but the tradition that he was a tentmaker survived in the early church and was recorded near 95 A.D. in The Acts of the Apostles 18:3. (2) He mentions the blameless manner in which he and his colleagues conducted themselves while in Thessalonica (2:10). And (3) when he wrote four years later to the Philippians he recalled that while in Thessalonica the Philippians had sent him financial assistance at least twice (Phil. 4:16).

How long does it take a person to establish himself effectively at a trade in a new environment? How long does it take for a new church to get to understand the good moral conduct and character of one who has been to them previously a total stranger? How long does it take for a church twice to send financial assistance to an apostle who has moved on to a new field of work and is now seventy-five miles away? What were the occasions for such generosity? Were they anniversary memorials of Paul's first appearance in Philippi? We would judge in response to these considerations that Paul would have had to work in Thessalonica approximately two years.

During this time Paul established a fairly satisfactory church in Thessalonica. His converts were gentiles, not Jewish people, as reflected in his letter: ". . . you turned unto God from idols . . ." (1:9). He was pleased with their growing reputation in Macedonia, Achaia and in every place, so much so that he regarded the Thessalonian Christians as models, types or examples for all believers in Macedonia and in Achaia (1:7-10).

The Acts of the Apostles 17:2 allows Paul three sabbaths, two weeks plus one day, possibly three weeks in Thessalonica. This brief amount of time would not be adequate for Paul to exercise his trade success-fully, for the Thessalonians to get acquainted with his blameless

morality and for the Philippians to send him financial assistance
twice.

After working in Thessalonica for approximately two years where
did Paul go next? Paul removed from Thessalonica to Athens, stayed
there only briefly, long enough to realize that he would have no success in Athens (3:1).

Very soon after Paul left Thessalonica what happened among his
converts? A disruption. Had Paul expected that problems would soon
develop? Probably not. His excellent experiences with the Philippian
Christians still echoed in his thoughts, and he could easily transfer
this optimism to the Thessalonians, so much so as to refer to them as a
model church. Did Paul learn of this disruption in Thessalonica? He
did. How did he hear of their problems? Probably from an itinerant
worker, one of those traveling workers so numerous in the church of the
northern Mediterranean world--apostles, prophets, teachers--informed
him of the disturbance, whom the Thessalonian Christians requested to
report to Paul soon as he was able to find him, or he could have
volunteered the information to Paul.

What did the messenger report? He reported that Paul's Thessa-
lonian converts were plagued with difficulties, and Paul found this
report somewhat disturbing. What did he do? Paul sent Timothy from
Athens back to Thessalonica with instructions that, since Paul and
Silas because of their fruitless efforts in Athens would soon leave
Athens and move on to their next stop, after his Thessalonian visit
Timothy is to report to him in this new location.

In his letter, which he wrote after Timothy returned, Paul mentions
Athens as the place of Timothy's departure for Thessalonica (3:1). In
the same letter Paul writes that Timothy has returned from his Thessalonian visit (3:6). He does not name the city where Timothy rejoined
him.

The author of The Acts of the Apostles is unacquainted with Paul's
movements immediately after he left Thessalonica, reporting that,
because jealous Jewish people created problems for Paul the brothers
sent Paul and Silas to Beroea at night. The Jewish people then pursued
Paul to Beroea, whereupon Paul was sent to Athens, Silas and Timothy
stayed behind in Beroea, then Silas and Timothy joined Paul soon after-
wards in Athens (17:5-15).

We are to regard Paul's account as the more reliable. Paul writing
within just a few weeks, or within a few months at the most, just after
he had lived through these activities, certainly knew what his movements were.

Why do we judge that Timothy did not report to Paul in Athens?
Paul refers to "all the believers in . . . Achaia" (1:7). Where are

these believers in Achaia? Are they in Athens? Certainly not! Paul was unable to establish a community of believers in Athens. Paul wrote I Thessalonians from a place in Achaia where he has enjoyed a degree of success, where he has accumulated a number of converts. Where was Paul, in what city was Paul, when Timothy rejoined him? It could not possibly have been Athens. The only other major city in Achaia where Paul worked was Corinth. His first converts in Achaia were the household of Stephanus. Stephanus lived in Corinth. Paul's later letters to the Corinthians verify his success, such as it was, in Corinth. Corinth served as his base of operation in Achaia. Paul's Achaian converts are in Corinth and the surrounding area. Paul is in Corinth where he has enjoyed a degree of success, has been there for several weeks, long enough for him to have made converts in Achaia, and long enough for Timothy to make his trip from Athens to Thessalonica and then down to Corinth where he rejoined Paul and Silas and reported on the Thessalonian situation to Paul.

As soon as Paul received Timothy's report on Thessalonica what did he do? Paul wrote a letter immediately, without any delay, to the Thessalonians as indicated:

. . . now that Timothy has come to us from you and has brought us the good news of your faith and love and reported that you always remember us kindly and long to see us as we long to see you--for this reason, brothers, in all our distress and affliction we have been comforted about you through your faith; for now we live, if you stand fast in the Lord (3:6-8).

Paul would liked to have visited the Thessalonians himself, but found it expedient to send Timothy instead, and hoped to return to them soon himself, but unable to do this and excited over Timothy's report Paul wrote the letter which we now know as I Thessalonians. His reference to believers in Achaia reveals that he wrote to the Thessalonians from his Corinthian environment.

Did the Thessalonian Christians write a letter to Paul first? We judge that they did, and that Timothy carried this letter to Paul. Where is this letter now? We do not know, and so far as we know it has not survived. We hope however that one day it will be uncovered, perhaps in Corinth, or, if Paul kept it and carried it with him, perhaps it will be retrieved in Ephesus. And if one day it is found we should hope further that it will be added to the canon of early Christian literature.

Did Paul write to the Thessalonians in response to this letter? We judge that he did. What did the Thessalonians write to Paul? We can speculate from Paul's reply that they wrote something to the effect, 'We thank God that when we heard the word of God from you we accepted it not as the word of men but as the word of God", which prompted Paul to reply:

We also thank God constantly for this, that when you received the word of God which you heard from us you accepted it not as the word of men but as it really is, the word of God, which is at work in you believers (2:13).

Paul's use of also, "We also thank God constantly. . ." seems to indicate a letter from the Thessalonians to Paul, and Paul is now responding to it.

The Thessalonians wrote further to Paul about "love for the brothers" locally in Thessalonica as well as for those throughout the region of Macedonia, to which Paul replied,

And concerning love of the brothers you have no need to have anyone write to you, for you yourselves have been taught by God to love one another; and indeed you do love all the brothers throughout Macedonia. But we exhort you, brothers, to do so more and more (4:9-10).

The Thessalonians wrote also of the return of Jesus, "like a thief in the night", to which Paul replied,

And as to the times and the seasons, brothers, you have no need to have anything written to you. For you yourselves know well that the day of the Lord will come like a thief in the night. When people say, "There is peace and security", then sudden destruction will come upon them as travail comes upon a woman with child, and there will be no escape. But you are not in darkness, brothers, for that day to surprise you like a thief (5:1-4).

The Thessalonians have demonstrated in their letter to Paul that they understand these things, and Paul notes that they really have no need to have anything written to them, which suggests that this is Paul's reaction to a demonstration of their understanding in their letter which Timothy carried to Paul.

What did Timothy report to Paul of the Thessalonian Christians? The church is in relatively good shape. However Paul has some enemies there, and his enemies have used his several weeks, perhaps a few months of absence to attempt to undercut Paul and to undermine their respect for him. Paul's sending Timothy only served to give them additional encouragement: Why didn't Paul return! Why did he send Timothy instead! What personal interest does he really have in you, his gentile converts!

Who are these opponents? They are unconverted gentiles, some of them undoubtedly and perhaps most of them indeed relatives of Paul's converts in Thessalonica, gentiles who found satisfaction in generating doubts about Paul among their converted relatives.

The Acts 17:1-10 gives the impression that Paul's opponents were jealous Jewish people, incensed by his preaching, who conspired against

Paul and his colleagues. Paul in his letter, contrary to The Acts account, is unaware of any trouble with Jewish people in Thessalonica.

Paul explains that his absence was as much pain to him as it was disappointment to them. He had hoped to return, found that he could not, so did the next best thing, send Timothy. The gospel came to them in power as well as in word. His accomplishments among them were adequate evidence to demonstrate the absurdity of those who assert that the gospel is a vain delusion. His conduct among them should make it all the easier for them to distinguish between the genuine, and the artificial imposter.

Paul explodes somewhat into a relatively sharp outbreak, doubtlessly annoyed by the irresponsible accusations of his enemies, aware that the Thessalonian Christians have endured unnecessary abuse from without, to compare this kind of persecution to that which the churches in Judea suffered at the hands of their own countrymen. While those who would disturb them have enjoyed no real success as yet Paul is much concerned about the situation, is very sensitive to it, regards the situation as a potential danger to the spiritual welfare of his converts, and uses a bit more than half his letter to refute their charges.

The sharpest difficulties in the Thessalonian church stemmed from these external disturbances, but the church also suffered from internal disturbances. Paul turns his attention to deal with them, to reemphasize his teachings which he had given when with them, and the remainder of the letter is a rebuke to the immaturity which some of them have demonstrated. He writes in summary after treating each of three problem groups separately, "And we exhort you, brothers, admonish the loafers, encourage the faint-hearted, help the weak, be patient with them all" (5:14). It is apparent from this letter that some of the brothers within the Christian community could stand improvement. Three kinds seem to be causing unrest within the church: (1) the weak (4:3-8), (2) the loafers (4:11-12), and (3) the faint-hearted (4:13-5:11).

Who were the weak and what was their problem? We are not to regard them as weak in faith. They were gentiles whom Paul had converted to Christianity in Thessalonica, but who had inherited Greek morals, and who consequently had little sensitivity to what Paul regarded as sexual impurity. Paul's Jewish heritage established him in the attitude of abstinence before marriage and fidelity after marriage. The Greeks in general, on the other hand, thought of the sex act as a natural act, gave it little forethought or afterthought, regarded it in fact as a very satisfactory way to achieve physical gratification. They had inherited many stories, some of them recorded by Homer, which related the sexual escapades of the gods. The object of the game was not to get caught by the party of the second part, and vice versa, and what was fun for Zeus was likewise fun for them. Paul is trying in effect to overcome their Greek inheritance. He solemnly warns them that their consecration to Messiah requires a very scrupulous sexual purity of life. God has not called us for this kind of uncleanness. He has called us in sanctification (4:3-8).

71

What one assumes is usually more important than what he expresses in words, and we wish we knew more about Paul's assumptions. We might well speculate: Was Paul married at any time before he wrote this? Did he have an unsatisfactory marriage experience? Did he project an estranged disposition about sex onto his teachings about Christianity?

What generated the nucleus of loafers within the Thessalonian church? They had heard Paul preach that the end of the world is near, that Jesus will return soon, that we are living in the last days. If Jesus is going to return before sunset today, indeed within Paul's own lifetime as he anticipated, then why should we be concerned about tomorrow! Why even work! Better to await the return of Jesus in exhuberant anticipation. This kind of retirement with all its leisure time created problems in the Thessalonian community. Who will feed, clothe and house them? What will be the reaction of outsiders, who are already criticizing them and Paul, to these irresponsible Christians? Paul was brief and to the point. He instructed them to get to work, to earn their own bread. Their idleness is a burden to other Christians and an object of ridicule by non-Christians. The church is not to feed them, not to assume any unnecessary burden which results from their loafing. They are to give up this fervor and excitement about an immediate end, take care of their own affairs in a responsible manner, and become an example of what Christians should be to those both within and without the Christian community (4:11-12).

What was the anxiety of the faint-hearted? Some of their friends had died since Paul left Thessalonica. They became disturbed as they tried to relate their grief to their recollection of Paul's preaching, convinced that these deceased friends would have no part in the great day when Jesus returns! Paul is very specific, relieving their anxiety in definitive fashion, by insisting: (1) Jesus will return, (2) the dead will rise. The Lord "will descend from heaven with a cry of command, with the archangel's call, and with the sound of the trumpet of God" (4:16). Those who are dead in Messiah will be given a kind of priority: first they will arise, and then all together, both resurrected and living, will be caught up together in the clouds to meet the Lord in the air, and then all will continue together with the Lord forever. But certainly they are not, like the loafers, to sit around and wait for this day because no one knows when it will occur. It will occur suddenly, unannounced, like a thief in the night, when everyone is complacent in peace and security, when it is least expected. Paul then encourages them to that purity of life which Christians should demonstrate (4:13-5:11).

Was Paul writing a letter which he intended for all Christians everywhere throughout the ages? We would think not. He was not even writing to all his own converts. He was writing precisely to the Christians of the city of Thessalonica, the capital city of Macedonia, and he wrote specifically to remedy immediate situations which they were facing.

Then what does Paul mean when he writes, "I adjure you by the Lord that this letter be read to all the brothers" (5:27)? He is simply indicating that he wants all the brothers in Thessalonica, the weak, the loafers, the faint-hearted, and any others to get his message.

Paul greets them simply and unostentatiously, stressing faith, hope and love as gifts virtuous for them to possess. He compliments them and gives thanks for them. He refutes the charges of his enemies, who are not members of the Christian community. He treats the specific problems of the Thessalonian Christians, urges them to purity of life and helpfulness in the spirit of love, and relieves the apprehension of those who are troubled by the death of their friends. After admonishing harmony and good order Paul closes his letter with a brief benediction.

II THESSALONIANS

Did Paul accomplish in Thessalonica what he intended to accomplish by writing I Thessalonians? We gather up the impression, reading through II Thessalonians, that he both succeeded and failed.

Wherein did Paul succeed? In three areas of sensitivity: (1) The accusation against him by his enemies, namely, a lack of personal interest in the Thessalonians, affirmed by the fact that he had sent Timothy to them instead of visiting them himself, receives no mention in II Thessalonians, which suggests that he adequately refuted this charge. (2) No mention of the morally weak implies that Paul's dictum to them had been satisfactory. Sexual promiscuity suddenly ceased! (3) The silence of II Thessalonians on the faint-hearted seems to indicate that their anxiety has been relieved. These matters no longer offer any disturbance to the Thessalonian community of believers.

Wherein did Paul fail to accomplish his aim? He failed, so II Thessalonians leads us to judge, to cure the defection of the loafers, so that he had to write a second time to neutralize, even to reverse an attitude which he had preached to the Thessalonians during his approximate two years with them, and which he had emphasized in I Thessalonians.

What had generated the loafers within this Christian community in the first place? Something which Paul had said when with them about the end of the world, reflected in I Thessalonians 4:13-5:11, and their impressions resulting from Paul's teachings. What had Paul taught about the end? Paul indeed believed and taught that the end is near. It will occur soon, any day. The Lord will descend from heaven with a cry of command, with the archangel's call and the sound of the trumpet of God. The dead will rise, and all together, those resurrected and those living, will be caught up in the clouds to meet him in the air. All will continue forever with the Lord. But when will Jesus return? And when will all this occur? The return is indeed near, the exact day is unknown, is unpredictable, but it will occur suddenly, in the midst of peace and security when it is least expected, like a thief in the night, like birth pains which suddenly come upon a woman with child, and Paul urges the Thessalonians to live in an awareness of the approach of that day.

How did the Thessalonian Christians react to this, a very soon though unpredictable return of Jesus? Some of them took it rather seriously, and proceeded to live as Paul had admonished them in an awareness that the parousia is apt to occur any day. And how can they as sons of light best accentuate and demonstrate indisputably the firmness of their conviction that Jesus will soon return? By quitting their work and living as if today is the day! By taking no thought of tomorrow! By making no plans for the future! Tomorrow, in fact all the future will be very well cared for, in which they will have no need for accumulated earthly possessions. Their finest demonstration is to give no expression to anything which even suggests or simulates a tomorrow. Jesus will return today!

These loafers became a problem in the church. Until the end occurs who will feed them? house them? clothe them? They became a burden to the Christian community.

How did Paul handle the problem in I Thessalonians? He compared these loafers to himself. Does an apostle who establishes a church, as did Paul in Thessalonica, have a right to live at their expense while with them? Indeed he does! Did Paul exercise this prerogative in Thessalonica? He did not! He worked night and day so as not to burden any of them. Do these loafers have a right to live at the expense of the church? They do not! Paul had the right but did not use it! The loafers do not have the right but are using it! What are the loafers to do? They are to get to work and, like Paul when he was with them, earn their own bread. If anyone will not work how are the others to deal with him? They are not to feed him. What did these loafers do with their leisure time? They became busy-bodies, gossipers, another sound reason for them to get back to work. If they persist in loafing and refuse to accept Paul's instructions, what is the Christian community to do with them? Have no company with them, yet regard them not as enemies, but as brothers.

What was the occasion for II Thessalonians? An adverse report. The loafers have ignored the instructions of Paul in his first letter, but merely continued in their negligence, still troublesome to others, still giving others undue burdens and worry, still bringing the disrespect of the whole community upon the church. Paul's letter did not convince them that they should get back to work because they regarded obedience to his instructions as a demonstration of faithlessness, a forthright denial that Jesus will soon return. So Paul finds it necessary to write again to neutralize and even reverse the near and unpredictable return of Jesus, hoping to cure their defection by showing how they have misunderstood and distorted his earlier statements.

What is this reversal? What does Paul appear to teach about the end in II Thessalonians 2:1-12? Before the end arrives it must be preceded by some rather specific signs. What are these signs? The rebellion will occur first. Then the man of lawlessness will be

74

revealed, the son of perdition who exalts himself over every God; he
will take his seat in the temple of God and proclaim himself to be God.
At that point Messiah will appear, expose this imposter for what he is,
slay him with the breath of his mouth, that is, destroy him. Those
whom the lawless one has deceived with his pretended signs and wonders
will perish with him. Whereupon the Thessalonians are instructed to
relax their expectation about an immediate end. The end is not near,
evidenced by the fact that these signs have not yet occurred. The man
of sin, the enemy of all that is called God, this servant of Satan,
has not yet been revealed.

Why has he not yet been revealed? He is being restrained. What
is this restraining agency? We do not know. We are unable to identify
it. There has been much speculation about it, and this speculation is
made most difficult because the lawless one occurs in II Thessalonians
2:6 as neuter, and then in 3:7 as masculine. It is someone or something
with whom or with which the Thessalonians are familiar. In any case
Paul appears to encourage them to return to their status quo patterns
of living until they witness these signs, which are indeed very easy for
them to recognize.

What is the major clash between I Thessalonians 4:13-5:11 and II
Thessalonians 2:1-12? Messiah will return very soon, at an unpredictable
moment, like a thief in the night, like birth pains which seize a preg-
nant woman, unpredictably but inevitably within the near future, as
opposed to the disposition that Messiah will return in the more distant
future predictably because recognizable signs will precede his return.

After explaining the signs which must precede the return of Jesus
a curious comment occurs: "Do you not remember that when I was still
with you I told you this?" (2:5), as if there is a long time span
between his presence with them and this letter. If Paul actually
instructed the Thessalonians during the two years he was with them of a
distant and predictable parousia, and certainly it would have been very
impressionable, then why would he feel compelled to write such a lengthy
description before questioning their memory? Would Paul have questioned
their memory? And why did he not review this to them in his first
letter?

It was not in keeping with Paul's disposition to inquire, "Do you
not remember that when I was still with you I told you this?" as is
reflected in his second letter to the Corinthians (I Cor. 5:9, 11).
Paul's disposition was to declare clearly and strongly, "I wrote to you
in my letter . . ." This curious statement "Do you not remember that
when I was still with you I told you this?" plus the unusual reversal
which it is designed to support gives rise to a very significant question: Did Paul write II Thessalonians?

If Paul actually wrote II Thessalonians what would have been the
time span between I Thessalonians and II Thessalonians? He would have
written it certainly 50 A.D., two or three months after his first letter to them, after I Thessalonians was delivered to them and after Paul
learned of its partial failure, while he was still in Corinth. The

time span between when he was still with them and this letter would have been relatively brief. And II Thessalonians would have been of his letters which have survived the second letter which he wrote.

Would Paul do an about face and in II Thessalonians 2:1-12 write to the Thessalonian Christians in terms which were a reversal of everything which he had preached to them for two years and contrary to what he wrote to them two or three months earlier in I Thessalonians 4:13-5:11? Paul wrote in I Thessalonians 5:1-4:

And as to times and seasons, brothers, you have no need to have anything written to you. For you yourselves know well that the day of the Lord will come like a thief in the night. When people say, "There is peace and security", then sudden destruction will come upon them as travail comes upon a woman with child, and there will be no escape. But you are not in darkness, brothers, for that day to surprise you like a thief.

Since Paul explains to the Thessalonians that they already understand times and seasons and have no need for him to write anything to them about these things, a second letter to them from Paul on these matters would be superfluous! And yet we have a second letter dealing with times and seasons. It is bordering on the absurd to think that Paul would tell them they do not need any such instruction, then write such a letter, and we think Paul would not have done this. Consistency was not Paul's most outstanding virtue, but he was not that inconsistent.

II Thessalonians 2:1-12 contains a viewpoint not only which is a reversal of I Thessalonians 4:13-5:11, but it is in fact incompatible with Paul's disposition. If Paul actually wrote II Thessalonians would he not have reflected a distant and predictable return of Jesus somewhere in his other letters? We think so. And yet this doctrine of a distant and predictable return of Jesus, predictable because it is preceded by recognizable signs, is not found in any of his other letters. Why is it not found elsewhere in his letters? It is not Paul's attitude. A distant and predictable return of Jesus is a later Christian attitude which sprang up near the end of the first century, and it is the very heart of this letter. If we remove it from II Thessalonians its absence leaves the rest of the letter empty, sterile and purposeless. The content of II Thessalonians 2:1-12 is the real reason for writing the letter and it is contrary to Paul's thought. He always insisted on an immediate, that is, a very soon and unpredictable return of Jesus, and he probably would not have initiated such a reversal.

Did Paul get emotional satisfaction by describing vividly and intensely the vengeance which God will impose upon his enemies? II Thessalonians 1:6-10 describes this vengeance with such delight that some critics regard this section as interpolation, that is, textual addition by a later editor. This kind of vengeance described in II Thessalonians is incompatible with Paul's attitude towards his enemies in his other letters. His enemies in Thessalonica are mild in comparison with those in Corinth and Galatia, whereupon we should expect his

76

impulse for God's vengeance to be even stronger toward enemies in Corinth and Galatia. But he does not wish the vengeance of God really upon any of them. This section, II Thessalonians 1:6-10, appears to be unPauline, and it is most doubtful that Paul would have written in this manner.

Was Paul acquainted with the idea that the day of the Lord has already begun? Certainly not. Paul always argues that the day is in the very near future. Yet, while the major interest of the author of II Thessalonians is to clarify the distant and predictable return of Jesus, he seems to be acquainted at the same time with the doctrine that the day of the Lord has already begun, and he has Paul writing in part at least to refute this claim.

Now concerning the coming of our Lord Jesus Messiah and our assembling to meet him, we beg you, brothers, not to be quickly shaken in mind or excited, either by spirit or by word, or by letter purporting to be from us, to the effect that the day of the Lord has come (2:1-2).

In addition to the idea that the day of the Lord has already begun another item stands out: the suggestion that they might have received or might receive a letter purporting to be from Paul. Did the Thessalonians receive a letter which was disguised as if it had been written by Paul saying that the day of the Lord had already begun? This seems to suggest that they might have received such a letter. How many letters did Paul write before he would have written II Thessalonians? Only one letter! Who knew that Paul wrote this one letter? Only Paul, his close associates, perhaps a few of his Corinthian converts, the Thessalonian Christians and possibly his Thessalonian enemies. Would anyone in Corinth or in Thessalonica, either friend or foe, write a letter like that and forge Paul's name? Probably not. Does this statement in II Thessalonians 2:2 assume that Paul was a volumptuous letter writer? It seems to carry this assumption. Would Paul in 50 A.D. after having written only one letter be known as a volumptuous letter writer? Never. When did Paul become known as a letter writer? At the end of the first century when his letters were collected. The author of II Thessalonians is expressing an environment compatible with the end of the first century. Paul could not have written such a letter in 50 A.D., neither Paul's friends nor enemies could have written such a letter in 50 A.D., and the Thessalonians could not have received such a letter in 50 A.D. because the idea that the day of the Lord has already begun is an early second century concept and was unknown in Paul's day.

Did the early Christians expect Jesus to return soon? They expected immediately, any day, to see him descending on the clouds of heaven. Did Jesus return? The soon and unpredictable return did not occur. And with each passing day did the Christians delay their hopes for still another day? This was their only choice under the conditions. The years rolled on: 60 A.D., 65 and 70 A.D., 75 A.D. arrived and still Jesus had not returned. What will be the result of always pushing his return into the future? Will some of them come to understand, before

77

another fifty years pass, that Jesus' return might well be in the somewhat distant future? Will others forfeit the hope completely? And will still others explain that Jesus' return has already occurred? And after these trends have developed will they be able to rationalize their adjusted expectations in such a way as to support them? This is precisely what they did. The disposition of a distant future return of Jesus is found in II Thessalonians, and his return will be preceded by recognizable signs, which suggests a post-Pauline date for this letter. By the time the Fourth Gospel was written, after 100 A.D., the Christians had begun to forfeit their hope for a future return, and even to suggest that their hope has been in error, because the appearance of the Paraclete was the fulfillment of Jesus' promise to return (Jn. 14:16). This means that the promise has already been fulfilled, the parousia has already occurred, Jesus has been here among us already for three-fourths of a century. The suggestion of II Thessalonians 2:1-2 that the day of the Lord has already begun demonstrates that the author is acquainted with this doctrine, that he is writing in the early second century, and that the author is not Paul.

The case against Pauline authorship becomes stronger when we examine the language and literary style of II Thessalonians. The vocabulary and phraseology are indeed Pauline. In fact II Thessalonians reproduces much of I Thessalonians, a great degree of it. But Paul's letters are more than words and phrases. They contain a pouring out of his warmth of feeling, his affection to his recipients. Paul was still, after only two or three months, very closely attached emotionally to the Thessalonians, and this flow of warmth and affection is totally absent from II Thessalonians. Would Paul have duplicated in paraphrase a second letter, copying its vocabulary and phraseology from the first letter which was sent just two or three months earlier and which proved to be a total failure on the one significant point which Paul is trying to correct? Would Paul expect a second letter, a letter which reverses his first letter on the one point which is the heart of the second letter and which copies verbatim much of the rest of the first letter, to succeed where the first one had failed? We cannot feature this. The Thessalonians would not have respected him for such an about face. And certainly Paul would not have written a letter which is so starved in emotion.

We cannot support the Pauline authorship of II Thessalonians. It is the product of a later generation of Christian thought. How, then, did this letter come to be written? After the Christian devotees forfeited their expectation of a soon and unpredictable return of Jesus, and developed the idea that Jesus' return will be distant and predictable, or that it has long since been fulfilled by the presence of the Paraclete, Paul stood in an unfavorable light because of his antiquated doctrine about the return of Jesus, and yet he was cherished and honored as a martyr. How can Paul be updated so that he is acceptable to these late first century and early second century Christians? By someone writing a letter, ascribing it to Paul, which lends support to the turn of the century attitudes about the parousia. And this is what someone did. II Thessalonians 2:3, 15 are warnings which are natural for a later writer trying to update Paul and put him in good light.

The salutation of II Thessalonians 3:17 is more superficial still:
"I, Paul, write this greeting with my own hand. This is the mark in
every letter of mine; it is the way I write". Does this appear to be
an authentication of II Thessalonians? It does. Did Paul authenticate
I Thessalonians in this manner? Certainly not. II Thessalonians would
have been only his second letter. Would he within three months after
he had written only his first letter which he did not authenticate
speak of authenticating every letter in this manner, three or more
years before any and all of his other letters were written, before he
even knew that he would be writing them? Certainly not. Did Paul send
his personal greetings in his own handwriting in any of his other letters? Yes, in two of them: I Corinthians 16:21 and Colossians 4:18.
Does he, in these personal greetings in his own handwriting, suggest
that he is authenticating these letters? Certainly not! What does all
this mean? The author of II Thessalonians was living after Paul's
letters had been collected, during the turn of the century, and he did
not know Paul very well. He was acquainted with Paul's letters only
superficially, and he deliberately ascribed to Paul something which
Paul did not write. His earlier warning against any "letter purporting to be from us" (2:2) is a conscious cover-up such as was never on
Paul's mind. Did Paul, after he had written several of his letters,
ever suggest that someone might forge a letter in his name? Never does
he suggest this. His mind was not operating within this kind of periphery. If the Thessalonians had received such a letter would they
recognize it as not from Paul? They probably would. Did they receive
such a letter? Probably not. But if they had they would have known
that Paul did not write it. Would it be feasible for Paul to arouse
their suspicion in advance, before such a letter was even produced?
Such a warning would be unwarranted. Where then should we look in
order to find this letter of which the author of II Thessalonians
warns? Could it be his own letter which we now know as II Thessalonians?
Did he attempt to duplicate Paul so rigidly and to claim authentication
that his attempt betrays his motive and reveals that he is covering up
his own forgery, II Thessalonians, by warning against forgeries? Our
criticisms of others whether subtly or more directly, with suggested
warnings about what someone else is apt to do, are often in effect an
index to our own inner self. The intrigue of the author of II Thessalonians is in effect a revelation of himself. Do authentic letters
need to be authenticated? Never.

This letter was not intended for the Thessalonian community. It
was intended for all Christians near the end of the first century who
might have occasion to read it. We do not know who wrote it, but we
are confident that Paul was not its author. We do not know precisely
when it was written, but the late years of the first century or the
early years of the second century are most probable. We would expect
it to have been written prior to the Fourth Gospel. We do not know
where this letter originated.

I CORINTHIANS (II Cor. 6:14-7:1)

Did Paul have any success in Athens? No appreciable success. After he sent Timothy back to Thessalonica, unable to evoke any favorable response from the Athenians, he stayed there only briefly with Silas.

The author of The Acts of the Apostles (17:16-32) writes a most unusual account of Paul's activities in Athens, the city which was indeed the intellectual heart of Greece and in earlier days of the Mediterranean world. Paul, by invitation speaking to the Areopagus, reported that he found in Athens an altar bearing the inscription "To an unknown God".

At no time in Athens or in any other Greek city did the Athenians or any other Greeks erect an altar in honor of an unknown God. The Greeks knew all their gods very intimately. Living with their gods was a daily experience for them, no barrier existed between them and their gods, and they were so close to their gods that no professional priesthood ever developed among the Greeks. Only when people are separated from their gods, when there is a chasm between god and man, are professional intermediaries needed.

The Athenians listened patiently until Paul finally got to the point: ". . . he will judge the world in righteousness by a man whom he has appointed, and of this he has given assurance to all men by raising him from the dead". This was the climax of Paul's comments, what the Athenians had been waiting for, and they got the message: "Now we understand. He is telling us about another one of those oriental gods".

Greek gods could not die. Death for them was impossible. They were incapable of dying. Oriental gods on the other hand passed through death but they did not stay dead. They resurrected from death. The Athenians now understand what Paul is telling them about, another oriental god, whereupon after understanding the point Paul was making they can disband and return to the normal routine of their activities.

How do we know that Paul was unable to establish a church in Athens? It seems reasonable to assume that had he been successful there (1) he would have stayed much longer, a year or two; (2) he would have had later contact with them through a visit of Timothy or Titus or Silas or himself; (3) he would have sometime have written to them, certainly in preparation for a final visit with them to receive their collections for the Jerusalem poor; and (4) he would have referred to them in some one of his letters to Thessalonica, Corinth or elsewhere.

80

When did Paul reach Corinth? He traveled from Athens to Corinth with Silas, arriving in Corinth during the spring of 50 A.D.

Timothy rejoined them in Corinth after his visit to Thessalonica, and from there Paul wrote his letter to the Thessalonians as we have already observed.

Did Paul intend to stay in Corinth very long? His fruitless and therefore brief and discouraging stay in Athens, combined with a messenger's report of gentile enemies in Thessalonica, probably set Paul's mood for Corinth, whereupon he anticipated only a short visit there. He thought that he would return soon to Thessalonica (I Thes. 3:11). But things did not turn out that way. He began to enjoy in Corinth a marked degree of success.

How long did he stay in Corinth? A bit more than eighteen months, almost as long as he had stayed in Philippi, almost as long as he had stayed in Thessalonica.

The Acts account of Paul's first trip to Corinth allows him one and one-half years there (18:11). It appears a bit unusual that the author of The Acts should allow Paul possibly two weeks in Philippi, two weeks plus one day up to possibly three weeks in Thessalonica, and then a year and six months in Corinth.

The Acts 18:12 states that Paul, during his first stay in Corinth, was brought before Gallio the proconsul of Achaia. We do not know the source of this information, whether Paul was or was not brought before Gallio, but if Paul was so arraigned The Acts provides us with one firm bit of information which enables us to determine a date relating to Paul's activities in Corinth. Gallio's proconsulship, as determined by an inscription discovered at Delphi in 1905, lasted from June 51 A.D. to May 52 A.D. Paul would have been brought before Gallio probably a month or two after Gallio took office in 51 A.D., and he left Corinth soon after this arraignment.

Paul's correspondence reveals the numerous problems faced by early gentile Christians, which in Corinth seemed to be worse than in most other places, and the manner in which Paul faced up to them both in absentia and on return to the scene. The Corinthians were rebellious, they were recalcitrant, but Paul was able finally to square them around.

Did Paul stay within the city of Corinth, or did he work in the surrounding area? His letters imply something beyond the city. He greets them as if greeting all Christians throughout the area: ". . . all who call upon the name of the Lord Jesus Messiah, in every place" (I Cor. 1:2); ". . . with all the saints that are in the whole of Achaia" (II Cor. 1:1). This leads us to judge that Paul preached and established churches throughout the area of Achaia as well as in its capital city Corinth.

81

After eighteen months, in the fall of 51 A.D., Paul moved on to Ephesus. Another year and a half passed before he wrote back to Corinth. Paul wrote to Thessalonica because problems soon developed. Paul wrote to Corinth for the same reason, though the problems were much different and he learned of them after a much longer time lapse. His letters to the Corinthians give evidence of certain raw situations, crude life predicaments which he had to measure up to with the Corinthians, a controversy with many facets which was alienating them from the great apostle to whom they owed their spiritual birth through the gospel.

Is our I Corinthians the first letter which Paul wrote to the Corinthians? In writing the letter which now bears the traditional title I Corinthians Paul referred to his previous letter.

I wrote to you in my letter not to associate with fornicators; not at all meaning the fornicators of this world, or the greedy and robbers, or idolators, . . . But rather I wrote to you not to associate with any one who bears the name of brother if he is guilty of fornication or greed, or is an idolator, reviler, drunkard, or robber--not even to eat with such a one. For what have I to do with judging outsiders? Is it not those inside the church whom you are to judge? God judges those outside. Drive out the wicked person from among you (I Cor. 5:9-13).

This makes it crystal clear that our present I Corinthians is not his first letter to the Corinthians. Paul reviews what he told them in his previous letter, as if it needed to be reemphasized.

Where is this first letter which Paul wrote to the Corinthians? It has not survived. However we are quite certain that a page of it has been preserved in what is now II Corinthians 6:14-7:1. In reading along through II Corinthians 6:13 to 6:14 there is a perceptible break. The thought pattern shifts. The subject matter changes. Reading on through 7:1 to 7:2 we find another jolt in content. Now go back and read 6:11-13, then skip over to 7:2, omitting this section 6:14-7:1 which is out of context, and the thought pattern fits together. What does this mean? A foreign page, a fragment from Paul's first letter to the Corinthians somehow got misplaced, finally to rest in this location following II Corinthians 6:13, and there it has stayed.

Read this foreign section, II Corinthians 6:14-7:1, and it is akin to the warning which Paul reiterates about his previous letter in I Corinthians 5:9-11.

We are suggesting very strongly that II Corinthians 6:14-7:1 is a part of Paul's first letter to the Corinthians. No doubt this first and previous letter to the Corinthians was prompted by a communication which Paul received from Corinth, a communication which spelled problems, possibly delivered to Paul by an itinerant, but the details of such a communication are now lost, as is also most of Paul's first letter to the Corinthians.

PHILIPPIANS

What were Paul's experiences in Philippi? He arrived there, his first European stop, in the early months of 46 A.D., with all the enthusiasm of one who has at last achieved approval from the Jerusalem pillars, anticipating ultimately in fulfillment of their request a satisfactory collection for the Jerusalem poor, building his first church on European soil, his first church by which he can demonstrate the good faith which the Jerusalem pillars have placed in him.

He reflected back, writing to the Thessalonians 50 A.D., on a degree of shameful treatment which he received in Philippi (I Thes. 2:2), but he does not spell out what this shameful treatment was. We suspect that it was imprisonment because Paul, writing to the Philippians from prison, makes a relationship to his Philippian experience: ". . . engaged in the same conflict which you saw and now hear to be mine" (1:30). The Thessalonians were acquainted with the situation, or he had acquainted them with it, so there was no need for him to belabor it further.

The Acts of the Apostles (16:12-40) reports that Paul and Silas in Philippi were dragged into the market place, accused of disturbing the city, beaten publicly with rods, imprisoned with their feet in stocks, and dismissed the next day by the magistrates with apologies.

Paul was emotionally attached to the Philippian church, had much personal affection for them, as the very personal and spontaneous nature of his letter to them demonstrates. Of all his churches, only from the Philippians was he willing to accept financial assistance for his personal use (4:15). He knew that they would not misinterpret his willing acceptance of their help.

How long did Paul work in Philippi? We would judge approximately two years. After he left Philippi at least twice they sent funds to him during his stay in Thessalonica (4:16). They also sent funds to him in Corinth (II Cor. 11:9). Again, when the Philippians learned of Paul's misfortune in Ephesus, they had not forgotten him. They sent Epaphroditus to stay with Paul as long as needed, and he brought to Paul additional aid. How long would it have required for Paul to establish this kind of rapport with the Philippians, one who was to them a total stranger and unknown upon his arrival in their city? We would judge that, at the very least, a minimum of two years would have been required.

The account of Paul's activities recorded in The Acts of the Apostles allows him possibly two weeks in Philippi. It is most doubtful that this would have been enough time for him to come to town as a total stranger and establish the good relationship which he had with the Philippians.

What happened to Epaphroditus while he was with Paul? He became ill, then recovered, and was anxious to return home because his friends at home had heard of his illness and were worried about him (2:25-28).

How did Paul react? He sent Epaphroditus back to Philippi with a letter. Why did Paul write this letter? To discuss theological questions which troubled them? No. To settle disturbances and difficulties generated either from within or without the church? Certainly not. Though he does have a word of warning about Christians who insist on circumcision (3:1-4:7) Paul writes merely to express his affection for the church!

What is Paul's situation? He is in prison. He is depressed. He has a weary desire to be free from the obstacles which his enemies are putting in his way. But in spite of all this he is so touched and encouraged by the affection and confidence of his Macedonian friends that his exuberance appears in every line, indeed every word. Here in Macedonia, in spite of all tribulations which he has endured, his labors have produced abundant results, and Paul rejoices because of it all, which is reason likewise for the Philippian brothers to rejoice (1:12-19).

Does Paul hope to visit them soon? He certainly does (1:26, 2:24). But he also has a desire to depart and be with Messiah. Is Paul getting somewhat aged? Is he worn down by the burdens which are imposed upon him because he is preaching the gospel? Will he be pleased at last to find rest? If he has a choice between life and death which would he prefer? He would prefer to be with Messiah (1:23-24). To see them again, however, also has its merits.

Paul exhorts the Philippian brothers to humility. Why? Because their enemies have given them an opportunity to suffer on behalf of Messiah, which is apt to evoke a bit of pride, but humility should be their course. Paul admonishes them to remember Messiah, who had everything but relinquished all; who unlike Adam did not put forth his hand to seize equality with God, but humbled himself and so was exalted (2:1-11). With such an example they should "do all things without grumbling or questioning" (2:14).

At this point Paul could well have ended the letter. The sequence for conclusion is natural: "Finally, my brothers, rejoice in the Lord" (3:1). But Paul goes on, his thoughts pouring out spontaneously, to warn them against Christians who teach circumcision, whom Paul fears will seduce his converts into practices which will nullify their freedom in Messiah. If they find themselves attracted by their claims, they are to remember Paul's own experiences. He had all these things as no gentile could ever hope to have them. He had them first hand. He might well have boasted of them. But he appraised them for what they were, counted them less than nothing, and gladly gave them up. The Philippian brothers are to follow his example, to be on guard, lest their loyalties to Messiah should become nothing. Their citizenship is in heaven. They are waiting for the Lord Jesus Messiah. What will he do to their body of humiliation? Conform it to the body of his glory. With such a citizenship, how shall they accept affiliation with those Christians who teach circumcision? As foolishness (3:2-4:1)! The physical body, the body of humiliation is not that important. What are they to do meanwhile? Stand fast in the Lord. Paul mentions Euodia and Synteche. Who are they? We know next to nothing of them, only that they are quarreling. The others must help reconcile them (4:2-3).

After a word of encouragement Paul seems again ready to end the letter (4:4-7). But still he goes on further to thank them for the gift not because it is extremely valuable but because it was prompted by their affection, to give his benediction, and at last conclude his remarks (4:10-23). How many times does Paul try to close the letter before he finally succeeds? Three times.

Paul's three attempts to close this letter are so marked that some critics regard Philippians as three different letters, or at least as fragments from three different letters.

Polycarp, bishop of Smyrna, wrote to the Philippians, "Paul . . . when he was absent wrote letters to you . . ." (Phil. 3:2). Was Philippians as we know it three letters which circulated separately in Polycarp's day? Probably not.

This letter reveals a magnanimity about Paul, the kind of person which we might wish to see reflected in all his letters. He writes:

Some indeed preach Messiah from envy and strife, but others from good will. The latter do it out of love, knowing that I am put here for the defense of the gospel; the former proclaim Messiah out of partisanship, not sincerely but thinking to afflict me in my imprisonment. What then? Only that in every way, whether in pretense or in truth, Messiah is proclaimed; and therein I rejoice, yes, and will rejoice (1:15-19).

Paul's genuine attitude toward those who would afflict him seems to be quite the reverse of the sadistic vengeance reflected in II Thessalonians 1:6-10. Of all his letters had only this letter survived our picture of Paul would certainly be incomplete, but this letter alone would require of us a favorable disposition toward his attitude, his associates, his work, in fact the very high quality of principles which motivated him. It is superb in outlook.

From what place did Paul write to the Philippians? Our judgment swings the pendulum in favor of the city of Ephesus, contrary to the attitude of many critics who identify Rome as the city of its origin. Why Rome? Paul said that he wanted to go to Rome (Rom. 15:28), but first he must carry the collections from his churches to Jerusalem. We are often unable to determine whether the author of The Acts of the Apostles is recording information which he has picked up from oral traditions in the church or whether he is filling in the missing parts by letting his imagination run riot. He has an interest in showing that Paul's desire to visit Rome was fulfilled, that when Paul was arrested in Jerusalem he appealed his case to Caesar, which would assure his voyage to Rome even though he went there unfortunately as a prisoner (Acts 25:11, 27:1-28:30). Philippians was written from prison (1:7, 17, 30), and many critics, influenced by The Acts report that Paul was in prison in Rome, settle easily on Rome as the place from which Paul wrote this letter.

Once the critics influenced by The Acts have settled on Rome they then find support for their claim within the letter itself: Paul's casual mention of (1) the whole praetorian guard (1:13), and (2) the saints of Caesar's household (4:22). This is Roman terminology, appropriate for Paul to use only in the environment of a Roman imprisonment, whereupon without stopping to investigate the meaning of these terms they quickly judge that Paul's own words in turn support The Acts report of his imprisonment in Rome.

What is a praetorian guard? In his use of "whole praetorian guard" Paul puts a Greek ending on a Latin word, which should have been praetorium. What is a praetorium? Is it a prison? What is a praetorium guard? Is it a heavy military or police guard in and about a prison? Unfortunately for the hypothesis that Paul was imprisoned in Rome this is not Roman terminology appropriate only for a Roman environment, praetorium has nothing to do with a prison, and praetorium guard has nothing to do with guards in and around a prison.

A praetorium is the residence of a governor. It is used to refer to Pilate's residence in Jerusalem (Matt. 27:27, Mk. 15:16, Jn. 18:28, 33, 19:9), and it is used to refer to the governor's residence in Caesarea (Acts 23:35).

A praetorium guard is comprised of those who guard the governor's residence, and "whole praetorian guard" is as appropriate for Jerusalem and Caesarea as it is for Rome. Paul's use of "whole praetorian guard" does not demand that Paul wrote Philippians from Rome. He could have used it equally and as conveniently to refer to the Asian residence of the proconsul in Ephesus who governs Asia, and of the guard which functioned at the proconsul's residence.

Paul's use of "whole praetorian guard" offers no stigma to Ephesus as the place for the origin of Paul's letter to the Philippians.

Paul writes further: "All the saints greet you, especially those of Caesar's household" (4:22). What is Caesar's household? Many critics judge that "Caesar's household" beyond any question of a doubt means Nero's palace in Rome, whereupon this greeting as well as the whole epistle to the Philippians had to be written from Rome. Does "Caesar's household" refer to Nero's palace in Rome? Indeed it does, but it is far more inclusive than that. What does "household" include? It includes the sum total of one's possessions and servants. It is not to be equated to the western concept of a dwelling, possessions within the dwelling, and the immediate family, and this assumption of the critics which imposes contemporary western concepts and customs upon a 54 A.D. Graeco-Roman society is their mistake. Is Asia and the proconsul of Asia included within Caesar's possessions and servants? Indeed they are, whereupon "Caesar's household" does not reveal Rome as the place from which Paul wrote this letter to the Philippians, and it does not exclude Ephesus.

Before Paul wrote to the Philippians two round trips have been made between the place of his imprisonment and Philippi: (1) Someone has delivered a report of Paul's misfortune to Philippi, and the Philippians responded by sending Epaphroditus to be with Paul. (2) News of Epaphroditus' illness has reached Philippi, and Paul has learned of their concern for him. Communication between Paul and the Philippians was fairly convenient and effective. Are two such round trips from Rome to Philippi, four-hundred miles one way, totally by foot except for two days each way by boat, reasonable? We think not. Rome was far removed, and such trips would have been most awkward, next to impossible. Communication between Paul imprisoned in Ephesus and the Christians in Philippi, a trip of two-hundred miles totally by boat, was, on the other hand, both convenient and reasonable.

Paul expects soon to send Timothy to Philippi (2:19), and then Paul expects to make the trip himself (1:26, 2:24). Is Timothy's proposed visit soon to Philippi reasonable if Paul is writing from Ephesus? To this we must reply in the affirmative. Is Paul's proposed visit to Philippi reasonable if Paul is writing from Ephesus? Again we must reply affirmatively.

Paul's proposed visit to Philippi is for the specific purpose of receiving the Philippian contributions for the Jerusalem poor. He visited all of his churches for this purpose. He turned his efforts to accomplish this errand upon leaving Ephesus, going first to Galatia, stopping at Troas briefly, then moving on to Philippi. His trip to Jerusalem with the funds was still ahead of him. To insist that Paul collected these contributions from his churches after his last trip to Jerusalem, that is, his last trip to Jerusalem as reported in The Acts, and after his Roman imprisonment is quite pointless.

We judge that Paul wrote to the Philippians during his imprisonment in Ephesus.

PHILEMON

How many letters did Paul address to a single individual? Only one which has survived, and that one is addressed to Philemon.

In this letter to Philemon, Paul also greets Apphia and Archippus. Who are Apphia and Archippus? We might assume with Theodore of Mopsuestia that Apphia and Archippus are Philemon's wife and son. They could have been, but no evidence was available to Theodore and none is available to us now by which we can demonstrate the reliability of this suggestion. It is only a guess, possibly a wish. Of them we know only their names, nothing more, except that Paul sends greetings to them.

Where did Philemon live? In Colossae (Col. 4:7-9). Had Paul ever been to Colossae? He had not been there when he wrote this letter, and we have no evidence that he ever went there. Where did Paul meet Philemon? He probably met Philemon in Ephesus when Philemon came to that city, and Paul succeeded in converting him to Christianity (19). Paul regards himself as on comparably intimate terms with Philemon, enough to request that he prepare his guest chamber for Paul's proposed visit.

Why did Paul write to Philemon? The purpose becomes very clear in the letter. Paul has become acquainted with Onesimus, who could well have been arrested and jailed in Ephesus, whereupon Paul would have met him as a fellow prisoner. Onesimus was Philemon's servant, who had run away possibly with some of Philemon's money (17-18). Paul succeeded in converting Onesimus, likewise, to Christianity, and seems to have developed a degree of admiration for him. Paul would be glad to keep Onesimus with him during his imprisonment, but insists, however, that Onesimus must return to Philemon. We are not to regard Paul as making a request for Philemon to release Onesimus so that he can become a companion worker with Paul.

How is this return to be effected? Onesimus will travel back to Colossae with Tychicus. Tychicus will deliver with Onesimus a letter from Paul to Philemon. Tychicus will carry at the same time a second letter to the Christians of Colossae (Col. 4:7, 9), and still a third letter to the Christians of Laodicea (Eph. 6:21, Col. 4:16).

How is Philemon to receive Onesimus? He is to forgive him for running away. He is to restore him in his confidence (10). If he owes anything to Philemon, possibly stolen money, Philemon is to charge it to Paul who will repay. Philemon is to receive him "no longer as a servant, but more than a servant, as a beloved brother" (16).

What does Onesimus mean? The "useful one" or the "profitable one". Paul could not by-pass the temptation for a note of humorous double-talk: the useful one "who formerly was useless to you, but now is useful to you and to me" (11).

Does Paul request the emancipation of Onesimus? No. This was not a problem, and certainly is not comparable to slavery as it prevailed in the nineteenth century western world. Anyone who had to work for a living was a servant of some kind. Paul merely assumed, as we do now, that earning a living by working either at one's own trade or for another is a respectable part of the economic and social structure.

COLOSSIANS

Who founded the church in Colossae? Epaphras. He lived in Colossae, worked also in Laodicea and in Hierapolis (1:7, 4:12-13), probably enjoyed more success in Laodicea than in Hierapolis (2:1), and also had more problems in Colossae and Laodicea than in Hierapolis. Paul writes with Epaphras' approval to Colossae and to Laodicea, but not to Hierapolis. Certainly if there was any sizeable Christian community in Hierapolis, and if they like their neighbors were burdened with problems, Epaphras would have had Paul write to them too.

Colossae was a bit more than one-hundred miles east of Ephesus, Laodicea about ninety miles east, and Hierapolis was three miles north of Laodicea. The church in Colossae was comprised exclusively of gentiles (2:13, 1:21, 27).

Did Paul's proposed visit to Colossae (Philm. 22) ever mature? We do not know if he ever really got there. He had never yet been in Colossae (1:4, 7, 9, 23, 2:1); and he wanted to go there, visit Philemon and check on Onesimus' possible debts to him as expressed in his letter to Philemon. Now he has a second reason. Epaphras has traveled from Colossae and sought out Paul in prison in Ephesus to get his advice on difficulties which he faced, disturbances within the church in Colossae. Paul's potential visit to Philemon presented a possible opportunity for him to lend further assistance to Epaphras by visiting the community of Colossian Christians. Meanwhile with the approval and guidance of Epaphras he expresses himself to the Colossians in a letter. If Paul later learned that Onesiumus when he ran away did not abscond with some of Philemon's funds, and if Paul learned that this letter to the Colossians was effective, then Paul's motives for this trip to Colossae would be eliminated except for a personal and friendly visit. We do not know if Paul's proposed trip to Colossae ever matured.

What occasioned Paul's letter to the Colossians? Epaphras is having difficulties with his church in Colossae and he needs Paul's help. What seems to be the difficulty? Teachers of false doctrines, that is, false doctrines from the viewpoint of Epaphras and Paul, have been assaulting the church. Paul is in process of sending Onesimus accompanied by Tychicus back to Philemon in Colossae. The request of Epaphras made this occasion appropriate for Paul to send a letter also to the Christians in Colossae, a letter designed to clarify the Christian disposition, to expose these teachers of falsehood and to warn the Colossian Christians against them. Paul writes immediately, even before Epaphras left for home.

Who were these teachers of falsehood? It is difficult for us to attach a name to them. They were unlike anything found anywhere else in the church during the middle of the first century. Perhaps we should best call them "errorists", as they are usually referred to, for lack of a better name. The source of our information about them is most limited. Where do we get our information about them? We get it

89

from Paul. Where did Paul get his information about them? He got it from Epaphras. Was Epaphras at odds with the errorists? Paul's letter makes it appear that way. If we want to know the truth about someone do we get it from friends or enemies? Friends are favorably disposed, enemies are unfavorably disposed, so both very possibly misrepresent, yet at the same time there is possibly a degree of truth in testimonies of both friends and enemies. Did Epaphras, at odds with the errorists, represent them accurately to Paul? Perhaps in degree, but we have no way of knowing. Did Paul make a trip to Colossae and investigate the errorists before writing his letter to the Colossians? Certainly not. For the sake of fairness and more reliable information we wish that he had.

How did the errorists regard themselves? We do not know, and we wish we had testimony from them. They probably would have given an impression of themselves somewhat different, indeed more sympathetic, from that which was reported by Epaphras, but sometimes even self testimonies need to be scrutinized with precaution. One does not always understand himself as he really is.

Did the errorists, as would be typical of any such religious movement, regard themselves as more religious than most, better Christians than most other Christians? Did they regard their way as the route to perfection in Messiah? We think that they probably did. But how did Epaphras and Paul regard them? Epaphras and Paul on the contrary regarded the way of the errorists as a displacement of Messiah. The best we can judge from what Paul, prompted by Epaphras, writes is that Epaphras and Paul regarded them as indulgers in spirit worship, a strange philosophy, and a semi-asceticism which gave ultimate license to an inferior morality.

Paul remarks of the "errorists" with disapprobation, "You were also circumcised with a circumcision made without hands" (2:11). He further notes festival, new moon and sabbath (2:16). If Paul had stopped here we would suspect that the errorists are Christians who are teaching Jewish impulses. But there is more to it than this. Paul warns against those who make prey of the Colossians through "philosophy and empty deceit, according to human tradition, according to the elemental spirits of the universe, and not according to Messiah" (2:8). Paul warns further against regulations, "Do not handle, do not taste, do not touch" (2:21), and he warns obscurely against self-abasement, which is a kind of false humility, the worship of angels (2:18), and new entanglements with the elemental spirits of the universe (2:20).

What does all this suggest? A group of religious people within the church at Colossae are promulgating allegiance to cosmic demons, subscribing to a mild asceticism with lax morals, and indulging in a peculiar philosophical speculation. They did not attack Paul nor his teachings. They probably did not even know Paul. They simply thought that the perfection of the Christian life is to be realized by adhering to their prescription. They are offering to their less fortunate Christian brothers in Colossae the completed message from heaven.

90

What did Paul recommend to the Colossians? No ascetic practices, no spirit worship, no philosophy is needed to complete the gospel. Separate your minds from earthly things, set them on things above. Destroy those earthly impulses within you, impulses which doubtlessly characterize the errorists, at least in degree and from the viewpoint of Epaphras: immorality, impurity, passion, evil desire, covetousness. Messiah despoiled openly and triumphantly all principalities and powers, bringing to us a complete salvation, an unqualified salvation. Messiah is the first-born of all creation (1:5), in whom the fulness of God was pleased to dwell (1:20).

After giving a few words of instruction to wives and husbands, parents and children, servants and masters Paul mentions the arrival of Tychicus and Onesimus, sends greetings from his friends including Epaphras, encourages Archippus, and closes the letter.

Did Paul write this letter? Many critics have insisted that Paul could not have written it, and their objections seem to be limited essentially to two.

Objection 1: Paul could not have written this letter because of the peculiar kind of "errorists" which the letter attacks. They are unidentifiable. We cannot relate them to anything similar in Asia Minor or elsewhere in or out of the church in the middle of the first Christian century. They are not Gnostics, because Gnosticism did not yet exist. And since we cannot relate them to anything which was occurring elsewhere in the church they are fictitious, in fact did not really exist, whereupon this letter is a fabrication.

Objection 2: The extreme Christology which it reflects is unlike that found in any of Paul's other letters, such as, Messiah is the "first-born of all creation" (1:15), the one "through whom and unto whom all things have been created" (1:16); Messiah is "the head of the body, the church" (1:18); the unusual and strange mention of Messiah as having made "peace through the blood of his cross" (1:20), and "in him dwells the fulness of the godhead bodily" (2:9). Such expressions and such attitudes do not exist in Paul's other letters. His thought is quite different. For example, in his other letters Messiah does not appear as the head of the body, the church, but rather Messiah is the sum of all Christians. An exception to this observation occurs however in Ephesians, a contested letter like Colossians where Messiah is likewise as in Colossians head of the body the church (Eph. 5:23, 32). This christology in Colossians reflects the thought of an age in the church quite later than 50 A.D., and Colossians is therefore a forgery.

In facing up to these objections we can judge only, in spite of the fact that this letter does not sound like Paul, that a situation existed in Colossae which was peculiar to itself, unlike that found anywhere else in the church before or since. Almost any situation is in effect distinctive, duplications are next to impossible, and certainly we judge that the Colossian church was disrupted by these unusual "errorists". Their very nature required Paul to assume a

91

rather strained christology. They are threatening the position of Messiah. Paul had to meet them on their own terms, which means there is good reason for Paul to have assumed peculiar attitudes not typical of himself. He appropriated their phraseology, key words and attitudes which Epaphras explained to him, their thoughts and their language, and applied them to Messiah, to show in their language the supremacy of Messiah and the superiority of normative Christianity. Paul could have handled this situation in no other way, and we cast our lots in favor of Paul as the author of this letter.

EPHESIANS

Did Paul spend any time in Ephesus? We know that he did. How do we know? Ephesus is the city from which he wrote his second letter to the Corinthians, indisputably so, because he refers to a distressing experience in that city, fighting with beasts (I Cor. 15:32), and he affirmed his plans to stay in Ephesus until Pentecost (I Cor. 16:8). Does Paul in any of his letters make any other reference to Ephesus? Nowhere else does Paul mention Ephesus, and had he not mentioned Ephesus in I Corinthians 15:32 and 16:8 any connection which we could make between Paul and Ephesus would be reduced to pure speculation at best. We have already hypothesized Ephesus as the place from which he wrote I Corinthians, his prison epistles which are Philippians, Philemon, Colossians and the one which we are now considering under the name of Ephesians. We also judge that Paul wrote II Corinthians, III Corinthians and Galatians from Ephesus.

How long did Paul stay in Ephesus? Paul worked in Ephesus, which great city was indeed the hub of Christian activity in the Mediterranean world, using it as his headquarters in Asia Minor, for approximately three and one-half years. How do we know that he used Ephesus as his headquarters for three and one-half years? How do we arrive at this figure? Since Paul gives such minimal information about himself in Ephesus our judgment is purely inferential, the product of putting together a few bits and pieces of information in as orderly a manner as we can muster.

What is the sequence of Paul's activities in relation to his stay in Ephesus? Paul probably spent several months in Ephesus, possibly six or eight months, then went up to Galatia and established his churches there. We do not know if he left Ephesus under duress, we do not know the cities where he worked in Galatia, we do not know how many churches he established there, and we do not know how long he stayed there. He probably did not work in Galatia as long as he worked in Philippi or Thessalonica or Corinth, and his activities there could well have required up to one year. If Paul did not go into Galatia and establish his churches there during an interim from the first part of his three and one-half years when he used Ephesus as his headquarters we are at a total loss to know when else he could have worked there. From Galatia he returned to Ephesus.

The author of The Acts of the Apostles places Paul in Ephesus twice, once for a brief visit (18:19), and again for a two year stay (19:1-10). The tradition that Paul was in Ephesus twice, the first time briefly and the second time for a prolonged stay, might have resulted from Paul's going to Ephesus and staying for a relatively short time, then going into Galatia to establish churches there, then returning to Ephesus for a longer stay. The author of The Acts knows nothing of Paul's imprisonment in Ephesus.

After Paul returned to Ephesus we judge that he learned from an itinerant of difficulties in his church in Corinth at which moment he wrote his first letter to Corinth, the very first letter which he wrote in Ephesus and sent from Ephesus. He had been removed from Corinth approximately one and one-half years before he learned of the Corinthian problems. Why had he not learned of them earlier? He was probably working in the region of Galatia, quite removed from Corinth and from the central arena of Christian activities, and so was out of communication with itinerant workers who visited Corinth--apostles, prophets and teachers--most of whom sooner or later visited the great city of Ephesus, the then crossroads of the Mediterranean Christian world.

At some point along the way Paul was imprisoned in Ephesus, from which environment he wrote his prison epistles Philippians, Philemon, Colossians and the one to which is affixed the name Ephesians.

Soon after he wrote his first letter to the Christians in Corinth Paul received a report on Corinth from servants of Chloe's household. The church subsequently moved to send three delegates--Stephanus, Fortunatus and Achaicus--to report to Paul in Ephesus on the problems in Corinth.

Why didn't they communicate with Paul earlier? Any attempt to communicate with Paul earlier in Ephesus would have been relatively fruitless because of Paul's interim in Galatia. And the only response which his friends in Ephesus could give to inquiries of Paul's whereabouts was, "Somewhere in Galatia".

In response to the Corinthian emergency Paul sent Timothy by way of Philippi to Corinth to do what he could to remedy the Corinthian situation, and while Timothy was in route Paul wrote his second letter to them, I Corinthians as we know it, to prepare them for Timothy's visit. Timothy reported back to Paul that his visit had been totally ineffectual.

Paul moved to action, made a stormy visit to Corinth himself to try to set the church in order, then returned to Ephesus.

No sooner did Paul return to Ephesus than that he learned of difficulties in his Galatian churches. Paul was in process of writing a bitter letter to the Corinthians, his third letter to them. At the same time and in the same mood he wrote to the Galatians. From Ephesus,

93

we have already surmised, Paul wrote I Corinthians, Philippians, Philemon, Colossians, Ephesians, II Corinthians, III Corinthians and
Galatians.

How long would all of these activities assuming that they relate
to his stay in Ephesus--a stay of several months in Ephesus, an interim
of nearly one year in Galatia, a return to Ephesus followed by imprisonment, a stormy visit to Corinth following Timothy's failure there, a
return to Ephesus plus the writing of eight letters in Ephesus--how
long would all of these activities have required? We judge that they
would have required a minimum of three years, and since Paul probably
reached Ephesus in the fall and left a few years later in the spring,
after Pentecost, three and one-half years is probably as accurate a
figure as we can determine for his stay in Ephesus.

At the end of his stay in Ephesus Paul planned to revisit all his
churches and, in fulfillment of the request of the pillars of the Jerusalem church when they gave him their approval to preach the gospel to
the gentiles, receive collections for the Jerusalem poor. Which church
or churches did Paul revisit first? We judge that first he returned to
his churches in Galatia. Does Paul say that he is going into Galatia?
No. Paul does not mention going to Galatia, but he does mention to the
Corinthians his instructions to the churches in Galatia regarding the
collections (I Cor. 16:1). Before leaving for Galatia he sent Titus to
Corinth to deliver his third letter to them, III Corinthians preserved
in part in II Corinthians 10:1-13:14. Titus agreed that he would hurry
on his way as fast as possible, deliver the letter to Corinth, then
travel by land up through Achaia, over through Macedonia, then on to
Troas, and try to get to Troas by the time Paul got there, to report to
Paul on the Corinthian situation; and if Titus did not get to Troas by
the time Paul arrived, Paul would follow a specified route through
Macedonia, probably through Philippi and Thessalonica, and somewhere
along this route Titus coming from the opposite direction would meet
Paul.

Titus failed to reach Troas by the time Paul got there, much to
the disturbance of Paul, who excused himself from preaching in Troas,
then turned to seek out Titus in Macedonia as he proceeded on his final
visit to his Macedonian churches to gather their collections for the
Jerusalem brothers (II Cor. 2:12-13).

While Paul was still in Ephesus, before he set out for Galatia, he
was undecided whether he would make the trip to Jerusalem himself along
with representatives appointed to carry from their churches, in addition to the gifts, accreditation letters, or whether, after the collections were made, he would delegate the task solely to the representatives chosen by the churches (I Cor. 16:3-4). By the time Paul had
revisited his churches, reached Corinth, and finished taking up all
collections, he decided at last to make the trip to Jerusalem (Rom.
15:24-28).

What kind of relationship prevailed between Paul and the Christians
in Ephesus? Paul used Ephesus for his headquarters in Asia Minor for

more than three years, staying there longer than anywhere else in Asia Minor, Macedonia or Achaia, and the Christians in Ephesus probably knew him better than he was known in any of the other cities where he worked. He was well acquainted and had many intimate personal friends among them, a tradition which was still vital among Christians a half century later and more. A very strong affection bound him to Ephesus, and he would have been writing to his very close friends and to people whom he knew well.

Is this kind of personal warmth, the kind which results from a prolonged association, contained in the Ephesian letter? To this we must reply in the negative. The salutation is brief and colorless. Paul offers no personal thanksgiving for them, but rather a long and emotionless praise to God for his choice of his people. He sends no personal greetings at the end, as if he is not acquainted personally with his recipients. In fact, there is scarcely a personal touch in the whole letter. Its most distinguishing mark is that it is very impersonal, relatively cold.

Had Paul ever visited the Colossians? No. Was he acquainted personally with the Colossian Christians? Only with Epaphras, Philemon and Onesimus, but he was unacquainted with the others. Yet his letter to the Colossians is warm, loaded with greetings, emotion and personal touches. In contrast his letter which bears the name of Ephesians, addressed to Christians among whom he is supposed to have worked for more than three years, is purely impersonal. It is a sermon, somewhat, a comprehensive outline of the Christian gospel: the greatness of the gospel, the greatness of the church of Messiah, precepts for Christian living. It would be much more appropriate for any group of Christians, particularly those whom he had never met personally.

This dichotomy, emotional warmth expressed to the Colossians whom he had never met, as opposed to the emotional frigidity toward the Ephesians whom we would expect to be his finest friends, gives rise to the question: Is Ephesians a letter which Paul wrote to his friends and acquaintances, his Christian brothers, in Ephesus? To this question we must reply in the negative. Why the negative? For reasons of (1) internal evidence, that is, content; and (2) external evidence found in the earliest manuscripts of Ephesians and in four of the Apostolic Fathers.

What is the internal evidence? Several statements in the text of this letter make the Ephesian destination for this letter impossible.

(1) ". . . I have heard of your faith in the Lord Messiah . . ." (1:15-16). Would Paul have written like this to the Ephesians? This statement is incompatible with his Ephesian experience. He is writing hearsay to his recipients, exactly what we would expect to total strangers, people with whom he has no personal acquaintance. He would not have written this kind of hearsay to the Ephesians, but would have reflected a very personal and first-hand acquaintance with them. This kind of statement is most inappropriate for the Ephesians.

(2) ". . . assuming that you have heard of the stewardship of God's grace that was given to me for you . . . When you read this you can perceive my insight into the mystery of Messiah . . ." (3:1-4). It is ironic, in fact ridiculous, to think that Paul would have to assume that the Ephesians would have learned this kind of information about him second hand. They would already be acquainted with Paul's insight into the mystery of Messiah as the result of associating personally with Paul for more than three years, and Paul would not have to assume this. These words in a letter from Paul to the Ephesian Christians would be in fact absurd.

(3) ". . . assuming that you have heard about him and were taught in him . . ." (4:20-21). Paul understood, in great degree at least, that the Ephesian Christians had heard about Jesus Messiah and that they were taught in him, certainly as much as anyone could learn of these matters in three and one-half years of personal association with them. Paul would make such an assumption only in relation to people who were to him total strangers. This assumption is simply out of place in a letter which Paul would write to the Ephesians.

(4) Paul writes further, "Now that you also may know how I am and what I am doing, Tychicus the beloved brother and faithful minister in the Lord will tell you everything. I have sent him to you for this very purpose, that you may know how we are, and that he may encourage your hearts" (6:21-22). Would Paul have sent Tychicus with a letter to the Ephesian Christians to report to them how he was and what he was doing when, even though he was in prison, he was readily and easily available to them in Ephesus? It hardly seems reasonable.

What is the external evidence that Paul did not write this letter to the Christians in Ephesus? The external evidence relates solely to the use of "in Ephesus" within the text (1:1).

(1) The two oldest manuscripts of Ephesians, the Chester Beatty papyrus and Codex Sinaiticus, do not contain "in Ephesus".

(2) The church fathers Origen, Marcion, Basil and Jerome were unaware that "in Ephesus" was in the text.

What does this mean? Paul, if he wrote this letter, addressed it "to the saints who are also faithful in Messiah Jesus". Paul would not and did not address this letter to the saints "in Ephesus". "In Ephesus" was added by a later scribe. The whole situation reflected in the letter, in the two earliest texts, and in four of the Apostolic Fathers dispells the Ephesians as the recipients of this letter. Paul could not have written this letter to the Ephesians.

To whom, then, did Paul send this letter? He wrote to the Colossians, "And when this letter has been read among you, have it read also in the church of the Laodiceans; and see that you read also the letter from Laodicea" (Col. 4:16). Is this letter which bears the name Ephesians in reality the letter which Paul wrote to the Laodiceans? Paul sent three letters by Tychicus when he delivered Onesimus to

Philemon: one letter to Philemon, one letter to Colossae, and one letter to Laodicea.

This judgment is purely inductive. Paul does not say, "Tychicus is carrying three letters for me, one to Philemon, one to Colossae, one to Laodicea". When would Paul have sent these letters? When he sent Onesimus in the care of Tychicus back to Philemon. Who is Paul's representative on this occasion? Tychicus. Who would at the same time carry these letters? Tychicus.

This letter is similar to Colossians. The contents are different but the outlines are fairly identical. The manual on Christian conduct, duties of wives, husbands, children, fathers, servants, masters are the same in both letters. Differences between the two letters appear in relation to Paul's personal touches. He was acquainted with Onesimus, Philemon and Epaphras, had learned somewhat of the Colossians through them, and even though he was unacquainted personally with most of the Colossians he could write to them with the personal touches of one who was an acquaintance and friend of their spiritual parent. Paul, probably because he was unacquainted personally with anyone in Laodicea, is more impersonal in the letter which bears the name Ephesians. Epaphras had worked in Laodicea but he lived in Colossae. These similarities and differences between Colossians and Ephesians are of such nature as to indicate that they were written at the same time, and cross references lead us to judge that Ephesians is in reality that letter which Paul wrote to the Christians of Laodicea, that is, if he wrote this letter.

Marcion, whose insights into Paul and his letters were unequaled by most if not all of his contemporaries, lists Ephesians in his canon as the "epistle to the Laodiceans".

For us to inquire: Did Paul write this letter to the Ephesians? is not enough. We must go one step further and inquire: Did Paul write this letter? This question is forced because much of the information and many of the attitudes reflected in the letter are diametrically opposed to Paul's disposition found elsewhere in his letters.

What do we find in Ephesians which is out of character with Paul? (1) ". . . built upon the foundation of the apostles and prophets, Messiah Jesus himself being the chief cornerstone" (2:20). What did Paul think of the apostles in Jerusalem, especially Peter, James and John? He blisters them in scathing terms, especially Peter during his visit to Antioch (Gal. 2:6, 14). His report on Peter and James is far from complimentary, the result of their refusal to give him the recognition he requested on his first visit to Jerusalem. Was Paul an apostle? He claimed repeatedly that he was. Would Paul who claimed to be an apostle and who had reservations about Peter the foremost of the apostles in Jerusalem urge this kind of prerequisite: ". . . built upon the foundation of the apostles. . ."? It does not sound like Paul. The author of Ephesians at this point sounds like he is writing long after the wider circle of apostles in the church had dissipated, to be replaced by the twelve, and long after the twelve had disappeared from

97

the scene, whereupon he is reflecting an age in the church which is much later than Paul.

(2) "When you read this you can perceive my insight into the mystery of Messiah, which was not made known to the sons of men in other generations as it has now been revealed to his holy apostles and prophets. . ." (3:4-5). Does "holy apostles", without dwelling on the fact that it is redundant, reflect good taste from one who is an apostle? We think not. This is more like the kind of thing one would write who did not consider himself to be an apostle.

(3) "And his gifts were that some should be apostles, some prophets, some evangelists, some pastors and teachers. . ." (4:11). Near the very same time when Paul would have written Ephesians he wrote to the Corinthians, "And God has appointed in the church first apostles, second prophets, third teachers, then workers of miracles, then healers, helpers, administrators, speakers in various kinds of tongues" (I Cor. 12:28). If Paul had written Ephesians would he not have made this list compatible with that of I Corinthians 12:28, especially since both letters were written, assuming Pauline authorship, just a few months apart! "Evangelists" occurs elsewhere in New Testament literature only in The Acts of the Apostles 21:8, written near 95 A.D.; and in II Timothy 4:5, written near 150 A.D. This term developed later in Christian vocabulary, and was unknown to Paul, whereupon it is most doubtful that Paul could have written using the term "evangelists"; and certainly he would have given compatible lists of workers whom God has appointed in the church.

(4) "In saying, 'He ascended', what does it mean but that he had also descended into the lower parts of the earth?" (4:9). The concept that Messiah descended into the lower world resulted from early Christian reflection on the role of Jesus in their salvation. Such a descent was not a new idea on the religious stage. Orpheus, Odysseus, Ishtar and others had enjoyed similar adventures. This idea assumed a Christian application to Jesus near the end of the first century and was probably borrowed from Ephesians by the author of I Peter 3:19. Since this is a late first century and early second century idea in relation to Jesus it is most doubtful that Paul could have written of it in Ephesians.

(5) The vocabulary of Ephesians is not typical of Paul. Thirty-eight words appear in Ephesians which are not found anywhere else in Paul's letters, in fact not even anywhere else in the New Testament. At the same time words in Ephesians used in Paul's other letters appear in two entirely different meanings, and synonyms in Ephesians for words used elsewhere in Paul's letters likewise assume two entirely different meanings. Paul uses "Satan" seven times in his other letters, Ephesians uses "devil", and the meanings are not identical, which strongly affirms that Paul did not write this letter.

(6) In addition to information reflected in the letter, and vocabulary, the style in Ephesians cannot be regarded as of Paul. Sentences are long and laborious, unlike anything in his other letters. Phrases

98

are heavy. Genitival formations appear, such as "strength of his might", "counsel of his will", unlike Paul in his other letters.

All these things add up to the very strong suggestion that Paul did not write Ephesians.

If Paul wrote both Colossians and Ephesians he indulged in a similar outline, the same moral code and laborious copying; and at the same time he indulged in subtle differences. For example: Messiah is head of the body the church in both letters, a similarity (4:16, 5:23, 32, Col. 1:18, 2:10, 19), but then differences occur. In Ephesians the church remains the body and Messiah the head of the church. But Paul goes on in Colossians to identify the cosmos as the body and Messiah as head of the cosmic forces. While we are aware that consistency is not Paul's most distinguishing characteristic this variance by Paul in two different letters which were written at the same time, carried by the same person, and delivered to the same general geographical area with instructions to the Colossians and Laodiceans that they are to read and then exchange these letters with each other appears a bit unusual and possibly a bit confusing to them. It seems rather that someone is devising Ephesians using Colossians as a source, and using from Colossians only that which fits his interests.

All these considerations tend to dispell Paul as the author of Ephesians. Another consideration however tends to swing the pendulum back toward Paul: if Ephesians was a forgery, not written by Paul, what would be the purpose of its author? He would have, in fact, no purpose at all; and the letter likewise would have next to no purpose. This gives us a weak case in favor of Paul as the author of this letter, but it is far from conclusive and it does not solve the problem.

What judgment can we make on the authorship of Ephesians? Paul possibly wrote this letter, and if he is its author he wrote it to the Laodiceans. A better understanding of the problems which Epaphras faced in Colossae and the relation of these problems to the church in Laodicea could well cast a bit of illumination on the unusual vocabulary and attitudes found in Ephesians. But until more information is available we expect that conclusive identification of the author of the epistle which bears the name Ephesians will remain unsolved.

II CORINTHIANS (I Cor. 1:1-16:24)

Where do we find Paul's second letter to the Corinthian Christians? It is now contained in the epistle which bears the title I Corinthians. When did Paul write this letter? During his stay in Ephesus, 54 A.D., in the spring before Pentecost, a few months before he left Ephesus to gather the collections from his churches in Galatia, Macedonia and Achaia.

99

What evidence do we have that Paul wrote this letter from Ephesus? In planning his final visit to the Corinthians, which visit will conclude his visitations to receive collections from his several churches, he writes that he will see them after he goes through Macedonia (I Cor. 16:5). He then goes on to report that he will stay in Ephesus until Pentecost (I Cor. 16:8). It seems that Paul is in Ephesus, that he is writing from Ephesus, and that he has not yet started on his collection tour.

Some would insist, however, that Paul is writing this letter from Macedonia: that he had been in Ephesus where he fought with beasts (I Cor. 15:32), that he left Ephesus to go to Macedonia during which absence from Ephesus he wrote this second letter to the Corinthians, and that he intended to return to Ephesus and stay until Pentecost.

Paul's statement, "I will visit you after passing through Macedonia, for I intend to pass through Macedonia. . ." (I Cor. 16:5) certainly does not imply that he is in Macedonia at the time when he is writing this letter. And the presumption that he wrote it from Macedonia fades away when we look at two other of Paul's statements to the Corinthians:

(1) He sends greetings from "Aquila and Prisca, together with the church that meets in their house" (I Cor. 16:19). Where did Aquila and Prisca live? A tradition placed them temporarily in Corinth with Paul as tentmakers, and greetings to the Corinthians from Aquila and Prisca by way of Paul almost three years after they left Corinth serves to verify their acquaintance with the Corinthian Christians. This same tradition removes them with Paul from Corinth and establishes them more permanently in Ephesus.

This tradition that Aquila and Prisca were tentmakers is recorded in The Acts of the Apostles 18:1-3, 18-19, 26. Aquila, so The Acts reports, was a Jewish person from Pontus, who with his wife Prisca left Rome because Claudius expelled all Jewish people from Rome, went to Corinth where they met Paul, Paul stayed with them, and together they worked at their trade of tentmaking, after which they moved to Ephesus where Aquila and Prisca remained and Paul went on to Jerusalem.

The fact that they lived in Ephesus is supported by the longer Epistle to the Romans, probably written to the Christians in Ephesus, where Paul greets a long list of his friends in Ephesus including Aquila and Prisca (Rom. 16:3); and by the fact that Christians in the middle of the second century were still aware that Ephesus had been the home of Aquila and Prisca (II Tim. 4:19). Paul writes to the Corinthians as if he has just talked with Aquila and Prisca, and certainly he sends greetings with their approval. They live in the city of Ephesus, and Paul is writing from Ephesus.

(2) Paul writes further, "The churches of Asia salute you" (I Cor. 16:19). He is writing certainly from Asia, specifically from his Asian headquarters, namely Ephesus.

How many letters did Paul write to Corinth? At least four letters. What do they reveal? The Corinthian Christians are indulging in a prolonged quarrel.

After Paul wrote his first letter, a letter prompted by information which he somehow received from Corinth one and one-half years after he had left Corinth, a letter which did not survive except for possibly a page now found in II Corinthians 6:14-7:1, Paul received some additional information, very disturbing to him, most disquieting, from servants of the household of Chloe (I Cor. 1:11). Where did Chloe live? Either Corinth or Ephesus. We should expect that her home was in Corinth, and if she lived in Corinth these servants were sent to Ephesus for the purpose, at least in part, of delivering a report to Paul. If on the other hand Chloe lived in Ephesus these servants returned to Ephesus from Corinth with the report. The Corinthian Christians, it is very clear, are having troubles.

Near this same time, that is, when the servants of the household of Chloe reported to Paul, three Corinthians--Stephanus whose household comprised the first converts in Achaia, Fortunatus and Achaicus (I Cor. 16:17)--arrived in Ephesus with a letter from the Corinthian church, a letter containing very personal and personalized information requesting Paul's advice on various problems. How do we know that Paul received this letter at the hands of Stephanus, Fortunatus and Achaicus? Paul mentions it several times in his reply: "Now concerning the things whereof you wrote. . ." (I Cor. 7:1, 25, 8:1, 12:1, 16:1, 12). Where is this letter now? We do not know. It has not survived. We have only Paul's reply to it.

We learned earlier that while Paul was in Corinth he received a letter from the Thessalonians. Did the Corinthians know of this letter and did it prompt them later likewise to write to Paul? A distant relationship is quite probably echoed here. We should hope that one day this letter from the Corinthian church to Paul will be recovered, perhaps in the current excavation of Ephesus.

Paul wrote his second letter to the Corinthians, which is now found in I Corinthians 1:1-16:24, in response to their letter to him. In the first part of his letter Paul deals with the information reported by those of Chloe. He rebukes the troublemakers. In the second part Paul answers the questions raised by the letter carried to him by the three Corinthians in such a way as to continue to rebuke the troublemakers.

Who were these troublemakers in Corinth? Their identity is obscured somewhat because we have no first hand information, only Paul's reply to reports which he received from their opponents. Paul's remarks in I Corinthians 1:10-17 give the distinct impression that there were four cliques within the church causing disruption: (1) the party of Paul, (2) of Apollos, (3) of Cephas and (4) of Messiah, and that Paul wrote to neutralize the resulting dissentions of a generally petty nature.

101

If we read on we find however that Paul does not condemn those of Paul and of Apollos: "I have applied all this to myself and Apollos for your benefit, brothers, that you may learn by us to live according to scripture, that none of you may be puffed up in favor of one against another" (I Cor. 4:6).

What does Paul mean by "scripture"? If "scripture" relates to the sacred literature which the church then possessed he would be referring to The Law and the Prophets. He certainly could not be referring to the Old Testament as we know it in the twentieth century because it was not yet compiled. Only its first two sections existed as a compendium. The Hagiagrapha was added to The Law and the Prophets in 90 A.D. by the council of Jamnia, thirty-six years after Paul wrote this letter to the Corinthians. He certainly could not be referring to the New Testament as we know it in the twentieth century because Paul was unacquainted with any such book; it did not exist. When Paul wrote this letter to the Corinthians he had written only seven of his letters; four of his letters were not yet written, and all of the other literature now contained in the New Testament had not yet appeared.

Paul does not speak well of the enthusiasts of Cephas, that is, Peter. Even though he received nearly ten or eleven years earlier what he interprets to be approval from the Jerusalem pillars he still carries a resentment toward Peter's rejection of him when he first went to Jerusalem (Gal. 1:18), and toward Peter's fluctuation in Antioch (Gal. 2:11).

These four parties in Corinth are not to be regarded as extremely important. Paul does not dwell on them and he does not mention them in his following two letters to the Corinthians. He uses this four-fold division, and exaggerates it perhaps, as a springboard to get to the heart of the problem. What is the source of the problems in Corinth? Those to whom he refers as "spirituals".

Who are the "spirituals"? Paul identifies them with those who say "I am of Messiah". The superreligious people gave Paul the most trouble. There is a suggestion that he had to contend with "spirituals" earlier in Thessalonica, and later in Galatia. We are not however to regard "spirituals" as duplicate problems in these three places. The "spirituals" of each place offered independent and distinctive problems, though they were no doubt alike on one respect: they regarded themselves as a very superior kind of Christian.

What distinguished the "spirituals" in Corinth? They believed themselves to be superior Christians because they were confident that they possessed superior spiritual gifts: utterance of wisdom, utterance of knowledge, faith, gifts of healings, working of miracles, prophesy, the ability to distinguish between spirits, various kinds of tongues, the interpretation of tongues (I Cor. 12:1-11). The possession of these gifts tended to give them a feeling of contempt for their weaker and less fortunate brothers who did not possess these gifts, and some of them even went so far as to belittle Paul for his deficiency in spiritual gifts. Some of the "spirituals" in Corinth, like the "spirituals" in Galatia, insisted that their spirituality placed them above the law, made them free from the law, which means in effect that they regarded themselves as having religious license to do as they pleased. In some cases they led flagrantly immoral lives, but they could do this without sinning because the possession of superspiritual gifts made them impervious to sin. They scoffed at Paul for being on a lower level of spiritual achievement, and who is therefore preaching foolishness in weakness, in fear and in much trembling. Paul was not surprised at such judgments against him because they reflected the normal dispositions of immature babes, those who while judging themselves to be "spiritual" have become nothing but victims of their own fleshly lusts, and they are justifying it under the pretense of being "spiritual". Paul makes it indisputably clear that to mature men his preaching is wisdom.

This visionary superiority of the "spirituals" led to a pitiful collapse of morals and created serious problems within the church. One "spiritual" was living with his stepmother in an incestuous relation which even their heathen neighbors abhorred, which is an ironic polarization because Christians by and large regarded themselves as living on a much higher plateau of moral achievement than that of their heathen neighbors. The other "spirituals" in the Corinthian church even took pride in the living arrangement of their incestuous brother because as "spirituals" they were above the law whereupon their actions could not be judged by social customs and conventional patterns of human decency. What does Paul instruct the Corinthian Christians to do? He wrote to them of this situation earlier in his previous letter, but some of them seemed to misunderstand his instructions, perhaps even deliberately misinterpreted his instructions. They are to rid themselves of lustful and licentious members. Certainly they cannot avoid contact with wicked people in this world, but they are not to tolerate them within their own group. Get rid of this wicked man, that is, do not allow him to continue within the Christian affiliation.

A second problem was taking a toll on the Corinthian church. Some of the brothers had become embroiled in civil lawsuits against one another. What an image of Christianity, Paul declares, you are giving to outsiders! But Paul can hardly deal adequately with this situation because his mind is stampeded by the promiscuous situation which continues to disturb him, and he declares that liberty does not give license to promiscuity. Fornication is a beastly, fleshly thing which defiles the body of Messiah, brings Messiah into unutterable shame. Christians are to turn away from fornication, and glorify God by their bodily conduct!

A third situation, compounded as it was but less serious in nature, about which the Corinthians inquired in their letter, is giving a degree of domestic consternation to some of their members, questions about marriage, celibacy, divorce, spiritual marriage, and the remarriage status of widows (I Cor. 7:1-40). Paul was unmarried and he recommended the same for others. He insisted rigidly on sexual abstinence for the unmarried and on fidelity of two partners after marriage, in either case the next closest thing to unscrupulous purity. Some of the Corinthians tried to relate Paul's recommendations, along with his comments about the end of the world, to their own situation, and needed his clarification. Should one get married? It is well, Paul instructs, for a man never to touch a woman, to remain single, but since this would tempt one to promiscuity each man shall have his own wife, each wife shall have her own husband, and so they shall live in the marriage relationship. If one cannot exercise self-control it is better to get married, and once married to stay that way. Divorce is prohibited, but if it should occur remarriage is permitted only between the estranged partners. If one is married to an unbeliever should he divorce? Only if the unbeliever so requests. What of virgins, those who have taken a vow of chastity, and yet, while really virgins, live with a spouse in a kind of spiritual marriage? A continuation of the spiritual marriage is preferred if one has self-control, otherwise the marriage relationship is permitted. Should widows remarry? Better to remain widows, but they can remarry if they choose. The sex relationship between married partners is the less of two evils, and in any case in marriage or out of marriage it is a fleshly, worldly thing. Paul emphasizes that the end of the age is near. Stay as you are if possible.

Still a fourth problem troubled the church in Corinth. What of meats sacrificed to idols? Meat for sale in the market was usually consecrated to some deity, and any Christian who purchased meat could not avoid using consecrated meat, so their inquiry concerned the use of any meat purchased at the meat market for dinner on a table in any Christian home. The Corinthians were largely gentiles who had been heathen religiously. Paul had insisted on a full and total break from heathendom. How can they break with heathendom if meat is still purchased for food? It troubled many of the Corinthian Christians. Does eating this meat however trouble the "spirituals"? Certainly not. They can do no wrong. How did their actions effect the weak? Many of them were disturbed by it, some were shocked, doubtless to the pleasure of the "spirituals" (I Cor. 8:1-13).

How does Paul answer the problem? Eating such meat in and of itself is an innocent act, because the deities to whom the meat is consecrated do not exist. But not all understand this, which lack of understanding might cause a brother to stumble, so that his conscience is disturbed, whereupon the stronger members should refrain from this action for the sake of another. A wounded conscience which one generates in another is an offense against Messiah. Liberty in Messiah should not be allowed to become a stumbling block for another. Forbearance, how your actions will effect others, becomes the measuring stick for the action which Paul recommends regarding conduct which relates to others, on a personal basis as well as on a social basis in the public gatherings of the church.

Paul then instructs women how to conduct themselves in the church meetings. When they pray and prophecy they are either to keep their heads covered, or cut off all their hair (I Cor. 11:6). He instructs the Corinthians further to correct the abuses which accompany their exercise of the Lord's supper memorial (I Cor. 11:17-34).

104

The license of freedom claimed by the "spirituals" led to a misuse
of spiritual gifts. Paul must clarify. There are many manifestations
of the Spirit: utterance of wisdom, utterance of knowledge, faith,
gifts of healings, miracles, prophecy, ability to distinguish between
spirits, tongues, interpretation of tongues. Spiritual gifts should be
exercised, however, with restraint. Why? Because spiritual gifts
edify others only when they prompt an intelligent exchange with others.
For example, prophecies edify others because the listeners get a message. Tongues edify only the possessor who exercises the gift, because
no one can understand, the mind remains fruitless, and to exercise this
gift is like meaningless noise in the air, aimless. It is better to
speak five words to the church which they understand, from which they
receive instruction, than to speak ten-thousand words in a tongue (I
Cor. 14:19). Paul stresses the fact that love edifies, and is the most
superior of all gifts from God. The "spirituals" speak with the
tongues of men and angels, but they should rise to a higher plateau,
cultivate and demonstrate the greater Christian gifts: faith, hope,
love.

For the "spirituals" who insist they are free from the law Paul
insists that their claim represents only a half truth. Of those things
which are lawful not all of them are helpful (I Cor. 6:12, 10:23). To
drive this lesson home Paul explains how he bypassed the law and refused
to take advantage of his apostolic prerogatives, to follow the more
preferably way, that of forbearance (I Cor. 9:1-27). One should sub-
jugate his own preference when doing so serves to help another.

Some of Paul's Corinthian converts probably wanted to know about
the resurrection, and Paul elaborates on this matter. At last he gives
instructions about their contributions for the Jerusalem Christians
(I Cor. 16:3), followed by a few remarks about his plans, the expected
arrival of Timothy, Apollos' coming to Corinth, sends greetings from
his fellow Christians, and closes the letter.

III CORINTHIANS (II Cor. 10:1-13:14)

Paul writes from Ephesus in the spring of 54 A.D. before Pentecost
in his second letter (I Cor. 1:1-16:24) to the Corinthian Christians:

I do not write this to make you ashamed, but to admonish
you as my beloved children. For though you have countless
guides in Messiah, you do not have many fathers. I became
your father in Messiah Jesus through the gospel. I urge
you then to be imitators of me. Therefore I sent to you
Timothy, my beloved and faithful child in the Lord, to
remind you of my ways in Messiah, as I teach them everywhere in every church (I Cor. 4:14-17).

When Timothy arrives, see that you put him at ease among
you, for he is doing the work of the Lord, as I am. So

let no one despise him. Speed him on his way in peace,
that he may return to me; for I am expecting him with
the brothers (I Cor. 16:10-11).

In writing his second letter to the Corinthian Christians Paul mentions
twice that Timothy is on his way to Corinth. Even before Paul wrote
he had already sent Timothy on a journey with instructions to go to
Corinth. Then Paul wrote in the letter, his second letter to the
Corinthians, about Timothy's projected visit, which he wrote after
Timothy's departure from Ephesus and which letter Paul expected to
reach Corinth before Timothy got there, a letter preparing them in part
for Timothy's arrival. Timothy did not carry this letter. It had to
be carried by someone other than Timothy. We expect that Stephanus,
Fortunatus and Achaicus carried this letter to Corinth.

How can we explain Timothy's earlier departure from Ephesus for
Corinth, as verb tense reveals, and a letter which Paul wrote after
Timothy left Ephesus reaching Corinth before Timothy arrived? Paul
sent Timothy on a detoured route, on an errand to Philippi, an errand
which would take him ultimately to Corinth. Writing just a few months
earlier, late 53 A.D. or early 54 A.D. to the Philippians, Paul explains:

I hope in the Lord Jesus to send Timothy to you soon, so that I
may be cheered by news of you. I have no one like him, who will
be genuinely anxious for your welfare (Phil. 2:19).

Is the trip which Timothy is making to Philippi a part of the same trip
which he is making to Corinth? We would judge so. Timothy has already
set out for Philippi. Paul then writes his second letter to the Corinthians. He wanted this letter to prepare them for Timothy's visit,
so he expects it to reach Corinth before Timothy. Timothy's errand to
Corinth by way of Philippi is adequate to give Paul's second letter to
the Corinthians, sent directly from Ephesus by way of the sea, ample
time to get there first.

Did Timothy fail to reach Corinth? Then Paul would have apologized
certainly in III Corinthians or in IV Corinthians, at least he would
have expressed regret.

Has Timothy meanwhile reached Corinth and returned to Paul? Yes.
Did Paul write his third letter to the Corinthians after Timothy's
visit? He did. Did Paul for the benefit of the Corinthians review
Timothy's report on them, or even mention Timothy's visit to Corinth,
in III Corinthians? He did not. Does Paul in III Corinthians even as
much as mention Timothy? He does not. Did Paul remain silent about
Timothy intentionally? We would judge so. Some of the Corintians
were filled with arrogance, puffed up, as though Paul were not coming
(I Cor. 4:18). The apostle who founds a church has the prerogative to
give instructions which the church must obey, so they were relieved to
have Timothy visit them rather than Paul because they were under no
obligation to obey Timothy's instructions. His visit, in view of the
psychological predisposition of the Corinthians, was doomed to failure,

and the Corinthians could easily afford not to be very deeply impressed by him. Is this why Paul remained silent about Timothy in III Corinthians? We think so. Did Paul ever send Timothy on another such mission to Corinth? Never. Whom did Paul send? He sent Titus on two successive missions to Corinth, and the "brother" with him, with an extremely high and at the same time extremely tactful recommendation (II Cor. 8:16-19, 12:17-18).

Did Paul ever again mention Timothy to the Corinthians? Only once. In 54 A.D. Paul sent Titus to Corinth to deliver III Corinthians, a scathing letter, with prearrangements to meet Paul in Troas. Paul meanwhile will take up the collections from his Galatian churches, and if they do not meet in Troas they will meet somewhere on a prescribed route in Macedonia. Titus rejoined Paul somewhere in Macedonia with a good report on Corinth. Paul wrote IV Corinthians, likewise delivered by Titus, in which letter Timothy joins Paul in greeting the Corinthians. After the crisis is past, and there is no further occasion for the Corinthians to resist Timothy, Paul appropriately brings him back into the attention of the Corinthians.

How many times did Paul visit Corinth? Three times. How do we know that Paul visited Corinth three times? Paul himself said so. He writes in his third letter to Corinth: ". . . for the third time I am ready to come to you" (II Cor. 12:14). And again:

This is the third time I am coming to you. Any charge must be sustained by the evidence of two or three witnesses. I warned those who sinned before and all the others, and I warn them now while absent, as I did when present on my second visit, that when I come again I will not spare them . . ." (II Cor. 13:1-2).

Paul has already made his second visit to Corinth. We know that Paul made his first visit to Corinth 50 A.D. when he established the church there. His third and last visit to them is still ahead of him, 55 A.D.

When did Paul make his second visit to Corinth? Paul had to make his second visit to Corinth in the interim after his second letter, after Timothy returned from Corinth to Ephesus with bad news, but before his third letter in July 54 A.D.

Paul's very first letter the Corinthians misinterpreted. Then Paul received reports from servants of Chloe, and from the three Corinthians Stephanus, Fortunatus, Achaicus, reports by which he learned that the Corinthian church was deteriorating rapidly. Paul's first impulse was to send Timothy to Corinth to assist them in solving their difficulties, which he did with an in route assignment in Philippi. Paul then wrote his second letter, a letter which would guide them and greatly assist them in working with Timothy. In this letter Paul anticipates a visit which will be most painful to them and to him:

Some are arrogant as though I were not coming. But I will come to you soon, if the Lord wills, and I will find out

107

not the talk of these arrogant people but their power . . .
What do I wish? Shall I come to you with a rod, or with love
in a spirit of gentleness? (I Cor. 4:18-19, 21).

I will give directions about the other things when I arrive
(I Cor. 11:34).

Timothy returned from Corinth to Paul in Ephesus with a most disheartening report.

Did Paul make this painful visit, his second trip to Corinth? He
certainly did, and he specifically states in his third letter: "I warn
them now while absent . . . as I did when present on my second visit,
that if I come again I will not spare them . . ." (II Cor. 13:2). And
he states later in his fourth letter: "For I made up my mind not to
make another painful visit" (II Cor. 2:1). His language makes it very
clear that he had been on this very painful visit, his second trip to
Corinth.

At the end of this painful visit, his second trip to Corinth, Paul
wrote III Corinthians.

How many letters did Paul write to the Corinthians? Four.

1. I Corinthians, the "previous letter", 53 A.D. or early
   54 A.D. in Ephesus. A page of this letter is possibly
   preserved in II Corinthians 6:14-7:1, and Paul refers
   to it in I Corinthians 5:9-13.

2. II Corinthians, found in I Corinthians 1:1-16:24, written
   in the spring of 54 A.D. in Ephesus before Pentecost.

3. III Corinthians, a "severe letter", July 54 A.D., in
   Ephesus, after his second visit to Corinth. Part of this
   letter has been preserved in II Corinthians 10:1-13:14,
   referred to in II Corinthians 2:4, 7:8, 12.

4. IV Corinthians, found in II Corinthians 1:1-6:13, 7:2-
   9:15, written November 54 A.D. in Macedonia.

It is noteworthy that the letter which comes to us under the title II
Corinthians is in reality a composite of three fragmentary letters, that
is, his first, third and fourth letters to Corinth.

In his fourth letter Paul mentions a very severe letter which he
had written "out of much affliction and anguish of heart" (II Cor. 2:4).
When did he write this severe letter? He wrote this severe letter just
after his second visit, the painful visit, and shortly before he set out
to revisit his churches to receive the collections. He sent this severe
letter to Corinth by Titus (II Cor. 2:13, 7:6-16) with arrangements for
Titus to meet him in Troas on his church revisitation itinerary and to
report to him on the Corinthian situation.

Paul was deeply disturbed for having to write this severe letter, and in his fourth letter he explains his anguish to the Corinthians:

When I came to Troas to preach the gospel of Messiah, a door was opened for me in the Lord; but my mind could not rest because I did not find my brother Titus there. So I took leave of them and went on to Macedonia (II Cor. 2:12-13, compare 7:5-16).

Is this severe letter preserved? Only in part. II Corinthians 10:1-13:14 is a fragment of this severe letter.

How do we know this? Read II Corinthians 10:1-13:14, and it stands as a separate unit, in the past tense of past disturbances which have torn Paul apart. He is weary. Dark clouds hang over him. His tone is heavy, severe, loaded with bitter scorn. Every reference which Paul makes to his severe letter (II Cor. 1:23, 2:3, 9, 3:1, 5:12) is an apt description of II Corinthians 10:1-13:14.

Now read II Corinthians 1:1-6:13, 7:2-9:15, and it too stands apart as a separate unit. But it is written in a warm present tense, orderly and coherent. The crisis is past. The dark clouds have cleared away. Paul is warm and exhuberant, in an exalted state of joy, because he has faced the ringleader in Corinth, his opponent (II Cor. 2:5-7), and it has resulted in a great success for the Corinthian Christians. The air is clear. The storm has subsided.

What does all this mean? These two sections of the letter which now bears the title II Corinthians do not belong together. II Corinthians 1:1-6:13, 7:2-9:15 is not an introduction to II Corinthians 10:1-13:14, and 10:1-13:14 is not the conclusion to 1:1-6:13, 7:2-9:15. There is an absolute chasm between them. They do not fit together, nor do they belong together as a single letter.

II Corinthians 10:1-13:14 forms a section of Paul's third and severe letter to the Corinthians, which we have identified as III Corinthians.

GALATIANS

How do we know that Paul wrote this letter to the Christians in Galatia? He addresses it to them: "To the churches in Galatia . . ." (1:2), and this is his only mention of Galatia in the whole letter.

In what cities did these Galatian Christians live? We do not know. Paul does not refer to any cities; he mentions no cities by name.

Does Paul make any mention of the Galatians as such? Only once, when, beleagured but not cut down, he addresses them "Oh foolish

109

Galatians!" (3:1). This appears to be a letter which Paul designed for circulation throughout all the churches in all the cities where he established churches in the region of Galatia, and their number was probably relatively small.

When did Paul establish these churches? We do not really know. If this letter had not been preserved critics would probably be engaged in an endless dispute revolving around the question: Did Paul establish any churches in Galatia? And what is the source from which we know that Paul had churches in Galatia? His second letter to the Corinthians. He writes to the Corinthians concerning the collections for Jerusalem that he will instruct them as he instructed the churches in Galatia (I Cor. 16:1). If this letter to the Galatians had been lost, and Paul had not mentioned to the Corinthians the churches in Galatia, we would not now have the slightest suggestion that Paul ever had been in Galatia.

The author of The Acts gives a very strange account of Paul's activities in Galatia, strange because he does not have access to any reliable information about Paul in Galatia, and is even confused on the location of Galatia. Had Paul's letter to the Galatians and his second letter to the Corinthians not survived no information about Paul's work in Galatia would have survived.

The Corinthians knew of the Galatian churches 54 A.D. But when did Paul establish them? Probably in early 52 A.D., certainly before 54 A.D., sometime early during the three and one-half years when he used Ephesus for his headquarters, during the one and one-half years before he was imprisoned in Ephesus. How long did it take for trouble to crystallize in Corinth? Approximately one year. Did it take somewhat the same amount of time for trouble to develop in Galatia? Very possibly.

When then did Paul move into Galatia? Probably in early 52 A.D. He reached Ephesus in the middle of 51 A.D., not earlier than the month of June, stayed for several months, then traveled to Galatia and established his churches there, but he did not have in Galatia such a prolonged stay as he had in Philippi, Thessalonica and Corinth.

When did Paul write to the Galatians? He probably wrote in July 54 A.D., immediately upon his return from his second and stormy trip to Corinth, at the same time when he wrote his severe third letter to Corinth, two letters at one setting, a severe letter to Corinth and another to the foolish Galatians, shortly before leaving Ephesus to take up the collections from his churches in preparation for his return to Jerusalem, and just before his visit to Galatia. The letter would get there first. Upon returning to Ephesus from Corinth, as if the Corinthian situation was not enough, Paul learned of the Galatian disruption. The mood of his third letter to Corinth is comparable with that which he wrote to the Galatians.

110

Is Paul on the defensive? Indeed he is, again. The letter seems
to indicate it: "Paul, an apostle--not from men nor through man, but
through Jesus Messiah and God the Father" (1:1). The Galatian Christians are plagued with problems, and in the process of dispute and
exchange among the Galatians Paul's apostleship and his not using his
office as bequeathed to him by the Jerusalem nucleus have been called
into question.

Does Paul compliment his readers for their spiritual progress, as
he usually does in his letters? No. He plunges headlong into his
rebuttal: "I am astonished that you are so quickly deserting him who
called you in the grace of Messiah and turning to a different gospel . . ." (1:6). Let all who preach a different gospel, which is in
fact only a pretended gospel, be accursed! (1:8).

Was Paul an apostle? He claimed that he was. Was he one of the
twelve? Certainly not. He didn't even know Jesus in the flesh. How
did he come to be an apostle? God chose him for this task before he
was born (1:15). Jesus then appeared in him in Damascus and clarified
this assignment.

Paul is unaware of an on the road to Damascus experience as
reported by the author of The Acts of the Apostles 9:3-19, 22:6-16,
26:12-18.

He went then to preach the gospel among the gentiles as it was
revealed to him. He did not receive it from the Jerusalem group.
After Jesus appeared in him in Damascus he went through Arabia preaching it and returned to Damascus, then after three years went to Jerusalem for fifteen days, his very first trip to Jerusalem, to visit
Peter, and he met also James (1:17-19). Then fourteen years after
Jesus appeared in him he went to Jerusalem again, his second trip to
Jerusalem, and even the pillars--Peter, James, John--agreed, so Paul
reports, that he was entrusted with the gospel to the gentiles (2:1-
10). His apostolic credentials are (1) God's appointment of him to
this task before he was born, (2) the risen Jesus clarifying this task
to him and (3) the churches which he has established.

When Paul was in Galatia did he preach circumcision? He must
have. How do we know? It is the recurrent theme of the letter (2:3-9,
12, 5:6, 11, 6:15). How did his converts react to this kind of preaching? It was to some of them a bit confusing because Paul preached circumcision with approval but he did not insist on it for gentiles.
What impression did this give to his Galatian listeners? This made
him appear to his Galatian converts as somewhat Jewish in sympathies,
perhaps moreso than he thought himself to be. The fact is Paul never
really forfeited his Judaism. What did they conclude was proper action
on this matter? By submitting to circumcision they would be following
Paul's recommendation and this would be indeed pleasing to him.

When Paul was in Galatia did he preach freedom? He must have because he writes an allegory about Abraham and his two wives, one slave and one free, explaining that Christians are offspring of the free woman (4:22-23, 30; see also 3:28, 4:26, 31). How did his converts react to this? Some of them regarded it as incompatible with what Paul had preached about circumcision. These two viewpoints are mutually exclusive. By preaching freedom, then approving circumcision for Jewish Christians and allowing it for gentiles, Paul appeared to neutralize the Jewish rite which he approves. They saw a conflict. To maintain circumcision is to negate freedom. To maintain freedom requires that they dispose of these Jewish hangovers. Which will it be? Circumcision? Or freedom?

What effect did these reflections on Paul's teachings have on his converts in Galatia? Disruption. It gave birth to two groups within the Galatian churches: (1) gentile Christians who think they please Paul by adhering to Jewish law, but who at the same time suspect that Paul by approving circumcision but not demanding that gentiles submit to it has proved false to the gospel entrusted to him by the Jerusalem nucleus. Paul replies that he did not get from Jerusalem the gospel which he preached, that he preached it for three years in Arabia before he even made his first trip to Jerusalem, that he did not receive the gospel from man nor was he taught it, but that it came by way of a revelation of Jesus Messiah. Paul writes in scathing terms: ". . . you who desire to be under the law . . ." (4:21). And again: ". . . you who would be justified by the law . . ." (5:4). These gentile converts comprised the Judaizers in Galatia.

(2) What was the second group which Paul's preaching generated in Galatia? Gentile Christians who insist on freedom, and who judge that Paul's gospel of freedom is neutralized by the Jewish elements which he allows. Paul refers to these as "spirituals", whose freedom has put them above criticism, and warns that their liberty must not be allowed to degenerate into license. Paul uses "spiritual" as an ironic designation, by no means a complimentary term: ". . . if a man is overtaken in any trespass, you who are spiritual should restore him in the spirit of gentleness" (6:1).

Who are the attackers of Paul in Galatia? His own gentile converts, largely one group, that group which reacted against the judaizing tendencies of some of their Galatian brothers, and who opposed Paul because of the Judaism which he promulgates while at the same time he preaches a gospel of freedom. They understood Paul as a dichotomy, in conflict with himself. He never really forfeited his Judaism, yet he is preaching gentile freedom from Jewish law.

What is the purpose of Paul's letter? He wrote (1) to correct the judaizers for their strained understanding of the Christian gospel, and (2) to refute the "spirituals" who were his active accusers.

Who were these judaizers? His own gentile converts to Christianity in Galatia. Had they become enamored by Paul's stress of certain Jewish practices, especially circumcision? It seems so. Did they think they were proving themselves faithful to Paul by practicing it? Undoubtedly they did. Did Paul appear to be strongly Jewish to his converts? Affirmative. What was the scripture which Paul stressed? The Law and the Prophets. Were Paul's moral requirements essentially those of the synagogue? They were. Were his Galatian converts now, by virtue of conversion to Christianity, truly "sons of Abraham"? Paul told them they were. These judaizers were gentiles; they are not to be regarded as of Jewish birth, but rather gentile natives of Galatia, Paul's own gentile converts, who claimed Paul's support for their actions.

Who were the "spirituals"? They were Paul's gentile converts who stressed the freedom which Paul preached, especially freedom from the Jewish law. Did they find their judaizing brothers intolerable? They certainly did. Had they accepted Paul's teachings? Certainly. Did Paul's note of freedom appeal to them? Without any doubt it did. What did freedom mean to them? Freedom from all Jewish ceremonial and legal restraints; and if one is not seasoned with a feeling for the more significant side of the coin, responsibility, what does freedom lead to? No moral conventions! The "spirituals" refused to be confined by anything. Did they claim Paul's support for their actions? They did.

Did Paul recognize in the judaizers a similarity to problems he had faced elsewhere? Paul saw reflected in them his earlier experiences with Jerusalem Christians during (1) his second trip to Jerusalem with Barnabas and Titus to visit the pillars, and in (2) his experience with Peter in Antioch and the arrival of Jerusalem emissaries from James. What does Paul recommend for them to do? Go ahead and get yourselves circumcised, but be fully aware that circumcision is nothing and uncircumcision is nothing.

Did Paul recognize in the "spirituals", those who insisted on freedom, a threat to religious freedom? He did. Freedom which has no self control gives license to promiscuity. What does Paul recommend for the "spirituals"? Get yourselves castrated! By making this recommendation Paul has in the back of his mind the cult of Cybele which was strongly established in Galatia, because the "spirituals" found in Paul's freedom a license to free sexual promiscuity, like the Cybelenes, and at the same time they believed themselves to be above the criticism of their brothers.

When Paul refutes the judaizers (3:1-5:10) he is thinking also of the "spirituals". After establishing that the proper appreciation of the Hebrew tradition does not imply bondage to the Jewish law Paul then returns to establish for the benefit of the "spirituals" the necessity of purity of life. "If we live by the spirit, let us also walk by the spirit" (5:25). And what does the spirit produce in us? "Love, joy, peace, patience, kindness, goodness, faithfulness, gentleness, self control" (5:22-23).

How many times did Paul visit the Galatians before writing this letter to them? Paul writes: "You know it was because of a bodily ailment that I preached the gospel to you at first" (4:13). What was

113

this ailment? We do not know. Does "at first" or "the first time" imply that Paul preached to them twice before he wrote? There is no way we can conclude that it does. On the basis of the Greek word "proteron" he could have made one visit, two visits or several visits before writing. There is nothing in this word which tells us, and there is nothing additional in the letter which tells us, how many times Paul visited the Galatians before he wrote this letter to them.

IV CORINTHIANS (II Cor. 1:1-6:13, 7:2-9:15)

What is the chronological order of Paul's actions as they relate to his Corinthian correspondence?

After Paul was in Ephesus approximately one and one-half years, during which time he also probably went to Galatia and established his churches there, Paul received news of a most disheartening situation in Corinth. If Paul had not gone into Galatia but rather stayed in Ephesus throughout this whole time he could well have been in communication earlier with the Corinthians. Soon after he returned from Galatia to Ephesus he learned probably through an itinerant worker of the distressful situation in Corinth. He wrote his first letter to them. Then came servants of Chloe with a report of difficulties in the Corinthian church, and soon arrived three messengers, a committee from Corinth--Stephanus, Fortunatus and Achaicus--with a letter for Paul from the Corinthian church and they sought Paul's help. Paul sent Timothy to Corinth by way of Philippi. Soon after Timothy left Paul wrote his second letter to Corinth, sending it directly and, to prepare them for Timothy's visit, expecting it to get there before Timothy arrived. Timothy returned to Ephesus with gloomy news for Paul. He failed to get the job accomplished. Paul set out for Corinth, two-hundred-fifty miles from Ephesus, probably late June or early July. The ringleader of the Corinthian troublemakers in the church has questioned Paul's authority as an apostle. Paul's visit was stormy and painful. He returned to Ephesus greatly disturbed, suspecting that he too, like Timothy, had failed, even to the point of no reconciliation, to the point of no return. He dictated a blistering letter, his third letter to Corinth. Titus delivered this letter, after agreeing to meet Paul in Troas, with the understanding that if Titus did not get to Troas by the time Paul reached that city they would meet somewhere in Macedonia in the routine of Paul's revisitation of his churches to take up collections for Jerusalem. Paul probably wrote to the Galatians at the same time he wrote this blistering letter to the Corinthians, with increased anguish because he learned on his return from Corinth to Ephesus that his churches in Galatia likewise had defected! A severe letter to Corinth, another to the foolish Galatians! Paul set out to revisit his churches. He doubtless went to Galatia first, fast on the heels of his letter, to visit his Galatian churches and then move on to Troas, which would give Titus ample time to deliver the letter to Corinth, then travel to Troas to meet Paul with his report on the Corinthians. But by the time Paul reached Troas Titus had not arrived. Paul was too greatly disturbed to preach in Troas, so he cancelled his appointment with them and went on to Macedonia. Titus rejoined him in Macedonia, probably November 54 A.D., with a good report about the Corinthian church (II Cor. 2:12-13, 7:5-16). The Corinthian Christians stand with Paul. The crisis is over. Paul wrote his fourth letter to the Corinthians, and Titus returned to Corinth with the letter. After revisiting his churches in Macedonia Paul then moved on to Corinth and stayed with the Corinthians for a few months before setting out for Jerusalem to deliver the collections.

Where do we find Paul's fourth letter to the Corinthian Christians? II Corinthians 1:1-6:13, 7:2-9:15.

What is its general nature and content? It is a victory letter from Paul and Timothy, an appropriate point to bring Timothy back into the focus of the Corinthians because of his earlier failure in Corinth. Paul relates the affliction they suffered in Asia, despairing even of life itself, feeling that the sentence of death was upon them. Paul wanted to visit them first, his anxiety was so great, then go to Galatia and Macedonia, then return to Corinth before going to Judea. But this agenda probably would have meant another painful visit, so he spared them. The ringleader who led the attack against Paul and disturbed the Corinthian church is to be forgiven, and the church is to comfort him. Paul's disturbance over them was so great that he was unable to preach in Troas. He writes of the spiritual freedom wrought by Messiah which leads to a denouncement of disgraceful and underhanded ways. Though afflicted, perplexed, persecuted, struck down, Paul and his colleagues are not crushed, not driven to despair, not forsaken, not destroyed. Paul is elated, exhuberant, refreshed, overjoyed. Titus has given a favorable report. Paul both regrets and does not regret his severe letter; even though it grieved them too, they were grieved into repentance. He writes of the liberality of the Macedonian churches concerning aid for the Jerusalem poor. Titus will engineer this work in Corinth and Achaia, so that all will be ready when Paul arrives.

It is possible that a small portion of this letter was lost in the process by which it became attached to his third letter.

ROMANS

To whom does Paul address this letter? He appears clearly to address it to the Christians of Rome: "To all who are in Rome, beloved of God, called to be saints" (1:7); and again, "So, as much as is in me, I am ready to preach the gospel to you also who are in Rome" (1:15).

Had Paul in his travels ever visited Rome? When he addressed his letter to them he had not yet been there, as he states in the letter: ". . . . I have often intended to visit you (but thus far have been prevented). . ." (1:13).

115

Would we expect, since Paul had never been in Rome, that he would be a stranger to the Roman Christians? Or would he have numerous friends and acquaintances among them? We would expect indeed that he would be a stranger to them. Yet at the end of the letter he sends personal greetings to a long list of friends.

Who was Phoebe? Paul identifies her adequately:

> I commend to you our sister Phoebe, a deaconess of the church at Cenchreae, that you may receive her in the Lord as befits the saints, and help her in whatever she may require from you, for she has been a helper of many and of myself as well (16:1-2).

And where is Cenchreae? It is the port city located east of Corinth. Paul recommends her to the hospitality of his readers.

From where is Paul writing this recommendation of Phoebe? We presume that he writes from Corinth, very close to Cenchreae, as Phoebe starts on a voyage. What is the evidence that he writes from Corinth? In writing to the Corinthians Paul indicated Corinth as his last stop in his revisitation of his churches to gather the collections for the Jerusalem poor; and these collections, which Paul made in fulfillment of the request by the Jerusalem pillars, would be completed with his final visit to Corinth. The collections are now completed, and Paul is ready to deliver them to the Jerusalem saints:

> At present, however, I am going to Jerusalem with aid for the saints. For Macedonia and Achaia have been pleased to make some contribution for the poor among the saints at Jerusalem; they were pleased to do it, and indeed they are in debt to them, for if the gentiles have come to share in their spiritual blessings, they ought also to be of service to them in material blessings. When therefore I have completed this, and have delivered to them what has been raised, I shall go on by way of you to Spain (15:25-28).

When, then, did Paul write this commendation for Phoebe? He wrote it from Corinth during his final visit there, a visit which lasted approximately three months, early in 55 A.D.

The Acts 20:3 allows Paul three months in Greece, and we judge that Paul spent most of this time in Corinth.

Then Paul proceeds to greet a long list of friends (16:1-27), and it appears that he has extensive acquaintances in Rome. Such a list of acquaintances is very unusual for a city which he has never visited, and raises the question: Is Romans 16:1-27 a part of the letter which Paul wrote to the Romans? All extant manuscripts, that is, all early manuscripts of Romans now in existence, have it. But we must inquire: Is this chapter suitable for Rome? And to this question we must reply:

116

We think not! Did Paul have that many friends, some of them very intimate friends, in a city which he had never before visited? Would we expect to find Epaenetus "who was the first convert in Asia for Messiah" (16:5) in Rome? Are Aquila and Prisca in Rome (16:3)? In writing from Ephesus to the Corinthians 54 A.D. Paul sends greetings from Aquila and Prisca; they are living in Ephesus 54 A.D. and Paul refers to them and the church that is in their house (I Cor. 16:19). The author of II Timothy sends greetings to Aquila and Prisca (II Tim. 4:19). Though it pretends to be a letter written by Paul from Rome to Ephesus Paul probably did not write II Timothy. It is a product of the second century, and the author is acquainted with the tradition which links Aquila and Prisca to Ephesus.

Paul closes Romans by sending from eight of his personal friends what appears to be greetings to the Romans. Are we to judge that his friends likewise are acquainted with the Roman Christians? We would judge that, like Paul, they are not so acquainted.

In between (1) the greeting to a great number of personal friends (16:3-16) and (2) sending greetings from personal friends to his recipients (16:21-23) is something most noteworthy: Paul refers to "the doctrine which you have been taught" (16:17). Is Paul acquainted in a personal way with this doctrine which they have been taught? He seems to be. Is Paul writing this kind of statement to strangers in Rome? Certainly not! Would Paul have any acquaintance with the doctrine which the Christians in Rome have been taught? We think not! Would Paul know anything of any teachers in the church in Rome who were creating dissentions and difficulties in opposition to this doctrine? Certainly not! Where did Paul's recipients learn this doctrine which they have been taught? Paul is so intimately acquainted with them and with the doctrine which they have been taught that we can judge only that they learned it from Paul. He is writing to a community of Christians who learned their teaching from him, and this kind of statement would be most inappropriate for anyone else.

If Romans 16:1-27 were isolated, separated from the Roman epistle, so that it stands alone, to whom would we suspect Paul is writing this last chapter of Romans? Paul is writing this introduction of Phoebe to his Christian friends in Ephesus where they live, who learned their teaching from Paul, and who are friends likewise of Paul's colleagues.

How did such a letter introducing Phoebe to the Christians in Ephesus get attached to Paul's letter to the Christians in Rome? To answer this question we must consider first the form and usage of Romans in the early church and then return to the question.

1. The bilingual manuscript Gg in 1:7 says "in love" instead of "in Rome", and in 1:15 it omits "in Rome" and makes no substitute for "in Rome".

2. The miniscule 1739, Romans, which was copied from the text of Origen's Commentary (extant now only in the Latin translation of Rufinus), bears a scribal note which states that "in Rome" was not in the original text by Paul.

3. The text of Romans which Marcion used was 1:1-14:23. Irenaeus, Tertullian and Cyprian often quote Romans 1-14. They never quote from chapters 15-16 where Paul warns against teachers of divisive and troublesome doctrines. Irenaeus could have made good use of this and Cyprian would have been delighted by it.

4. Clement of Alexandria and Origen are the only ante-Nicene (before 325 A.D.) fathers who quote from Romans 15-16.

5. In some of the longer manuscripts, those which are comprised of all sixteen chapters, the doxology is found twice, both after 14:23 and after 16:24; in others it is found only at the end, 16:25-27; and in still others it is omitted entirely.

What judgments are we forced to make from this information about the form and usage of Romans in the early church?

1. Romans existed in a short form comprised of chapters 1-14, sometimes without the doxology and sometimes with the doxology, with no mention of "Rome" in 1:7 and 1:15 and without chapters 15-16. In this hypothetical short text of Romans the doxology when it appeared was affixed at the end following 14:23 probably as an editorial addition. No copy of this short text of Romans has survived, but undoubtedly it did exist and was widely used.

2. Romans existed in a long form comprised of 1:1-15:33 with chapter 16 omitted, and in another long form comprised of 1:1-14:23, 16:1-27 with chapter 15 omitted, and in a third long form of all 16 chapters.

What does all this mean? It means that four versions of Romans existed and were used in the church from a very early date.

Paul arrives at last in Corinth. The church has meanwhile got in step with Paul's instructions, so that his problems in Corinth are resolved and in effect dissolved. But how are things in Ephesus? Ephesus, harried by opponents (Rom. 16:17) as most of his churches were soon after he left them, needed a sober word of encouragement and instruction.

Paul wrote Romans 1:1-14:23, making several copies of it, one for the Christians in Ephesus (there was a tradition that he wrote a letter to Ephesus, and we have already learned that the Laodicean letter somehow got titled Ephesians), and others for the neighboring cities in Asia Minor. He possibly also prepared copies of this letter for his churches in Galatia and he might have prepared copies of it also for Philippi and Thessalonica. It was a kind of farewell to all his churches.

Phoebe delivered this letter to Ephesus and carried with her the copies intended for the churches of Asia Minor, Galatia and the other places.

And now we are ready to return to the question: How did such a letter introducing Phoebe to Christians in Ephesus get attached to Paul's letter which is addressed to the Christians in Rome? To the letter for the Ephesian church Paul appended chapter 16 to introduce Phoebe, to greet his Ephesian friends, and to send greetings from his colleagues.

At the same time Paul wanted to write to Rome. What letter is more appropriate for them than this one which he has just prepared for the churches in Asia Minor! He directs Tertius his secretary to make another copy with two distinct references to Rome, to which Paul adds chapter 15 to stress the mutual responsibilities of Christians and to make clear his reason for visiting Rome. He omits chapter 16 in this copy which he sends to the Roman Christians because the introduction of Phoebe with subsequent greetings would be meaningless to the Romans.

We are, of course, merely theorizing on these matters. This explanation, however, demonstrates very clearly how four different versions of Paul's letters to the Romans circulated in the church from a very early date.

Does this letter give any insights into the nature of the Roman church? It certainly does not. Was it, then, designed with Rome in mind? It was not! But it was, nevertheless, a very excellent letter for Paul to send to the Romans, the very finest statement on the essence of Christianity which he ever produced.

Paul opens the letter with a salutation, words of greeting and thanksgiving. He is obligated to preach the gospel (and desires to preach it in Rome). What is the gospel? It is the power of God unto salvation.

Then Paul plunges in (1) to explain the mystery of salvation and (2) to exhort his recipients to right living.

Salvation is offered to all, and there is no other way. All men are under the wrath of God because of their wickedness. This applies equally to gentiles and to Jewish people. The Jewish people had the law to warn them, but the gentiles were without it. The gentiles had, however, something else, their conscience as an unwritten law which gave them the ability to recognize their moral obligations. Both the law of the Jewish people and the conscience of the gentiles have failed. But all is not lost, because redemption is possible through the Son's death, through faith in him and the consequent new life in Messiah. Redemption through Jesus does not negate the law; it establishes the law, because Abraham was justified by faith, and circumcision sealed the covenant given in faith. The gentiles have reason to rejoice because the warring of their conscience is ended, and they can now appropriate the safety and joy which the assurance of Messiah provides. The Jewish people have reason to rejoice. They were rejected. Why were they rejected? Because of their own unbelief. They attempted to achieve through works rather than through faith. They misunderstood, and so were disobedient. Not all of Israel was destroyed, however. A faithful remnant has been chosen

119

out, and the Jewish people have reason to rejoice because their rejection was only temporary. God has used Israel's failure to bring in the gentiles, and it is still possible for Israel to be saved. He warns the Christians, as a wild olive grafted onto the old stump, that if God spared not the natural branches neither will he spare you.

The capstone of Paul's argument is to be found in his exhortation to right living. Since God has provided this way at such infinite cost to himself man shall live in a fitting and proper way. His admonitions are short, brisk, crisp. He adds the imminence of the final great day as a spur to righteous living. He speaks of the strong and the weak in giving instruction about the kind of food Christians should eat.

His admonitions are concerned with the morality which is involved. His rule for Christian interrelations is forbearance, and this is the great principle which evolves from his teachings as constituting the heart of Christian living. He clarified it for the Corinthians when instructing them about eating meat which was sacrificed to idols, and he finds it expedient to emphasize it again in this his greatest of letters. One should not perform actions which keep a brother away from Messiah. And the weak should not become critics of the strong.

Paul goes on to inform the Roman Christians of his plans to visit them, and the reason for his writing. He closes with appropriate greetings and warnings against strife. The doxology, if attached to the long form 1:1-15:33, the letter which he sent to Rome, is probably liturgical and was added by a later scribe.

THE PASTORAL EPISTLES

A study of Paul's letters would be complete if we stopped with Romans. But we would at the same time loose something of Paul in the traditions of the church if we do not give consideration to three brief treatises, I Timothy, II Timothy and Titus, which appear in their design to be letters from Paul. For almost two-hundred years in western Christendom these three treatises have been known as the Pastoral Epistles.

Paul was probably martyred, and martyrdom was one way to gain esteem. Traditions developed. Near 90 A.D. the church at Ephesus probably collected his letters into a compendium, which made it easy for him to become known for the letters which he wrote to his churches. Soon thereafter the author of The Acts of the Apostles accessed his apostleship to paramount proportions, and by the end of the first century Paul was discovered by the church as a great letter writer and as the great apostle to the gentiles. By 150 A.D. selections from his letters, as well as selections from the gospels, were read in the Christian assemblies following readings from The Law and the Prophets.

120

Followed a revival of interest in Paul. Some in the church attempted to copy him, others updated his antiquated doctrines to make him more acceptable to the church in a new age, still others wrote to instruct the churches, and in all cases they lent authenticity to their treatises by making it appear that Paul was indeed the author. Such pretenses were exceptions rather than the rule, and we have judged earlier that II Thessalonians was such an attempt with noble motive near the end of the first century. Possibly very soon thereafter, but not more than seventy-five years later, the three Pastoral Epistles appeared. At some time thereafter someone in the early church tried to account for Paul's letter to the Christians of Laodicea by creating Laodiceans. And since Paul referred to Caesar's household in writing to the Philippians (Phil. 4:22), still another well intentioned person, probably judging Seneca to be a member of Caesar's household, devised a letter from Paul to Seneca, along with Seneca's reply to Paul. Still later someone romanticized Paul by producing The Acts of Paul and Thecla, possibly by one who was acquainted with II Timothy.

Paul was not known in the church in his own day as a letter writer, except sporadically by the churches to whom he wrote. All his letters except one were written during the last two years of his life. The six attempts to copy him, update him and instruct the church in his name--II Thessalonians, I Timothy, II Timothy, Titus, Laodiceans and Paul's letter to Seneca--occurred in the early second century and following, after he had become known in the church as a letter writer.

Our interest here is limited to the Pastoral Epistles, simply because they are included within the canon of early Christian literature and because they reflect in part what the early church made of Paul through traditions.

I Timothy.--Do we get the idea that I Timothy is a letter from Paul to Timothy? We easily get this idea (1:2), with the additional impulse that Paul hoping to visit Timothy soon might be delayed, so he writes a letter to inform Timothy how one should behave in the household of God (3:15).

But does this little treatise represent an actual situation in which Paul is writing a letter to Timothy? We think not. How long did Timothy actually work with Paul? At least nine years in Macedonia, Achaia and Asia Minor. Where does it appear that Timothy is now working? In Ephesus.

If Paul after nine or more years with Timothy actually left him in charge of the church in Ephesus is Timothy at this point in desperate need to be instructed so he will know how one should conduct himself in the church? We think not, and to think that he is in such need might even be absurd. But Paul proceeds nevertheless, or so it appears, to instruct him in spite of the fact that he left him in charge of the church in Ephesus as if he is writing to a youngster who has not yet grown up. The author is aware that Paul advised the Corinthians not to despise Timothy who was Paul's beloved and faithful child in the Lord

121

(I Cor. 16:11, 4:17), whereupon he projects the youth of Timothy into his instructions to Timothy but at the same time expects Timothy to conduct himself and lead the church as if he is a well seasoned out and aged adult.

Must Timothy reject all false doctrines, unmask the wicked and foolish teachers who are causing moral and spiritual pestilence in the church (6:2-5)? Did false doctrines bring spiritual havoc to Hymenaeus and Alexander (1:19-20)? Must Timothy stop the mouths of vain talkers and deceivers (1:6-7)? Must Timothy clarify rules of moral conduct which will insure good living and good speech (1:3-11, 2:8-15)? Must Timothy oversee the election of men and women who will be leaders in the Christian community of Ephesus, men and women who are pure of life and sound in doctrine (3:1-13)? Must Timothy guard what has been entrusted to him, and set an example for others by his own temperance, sobriety and orthodoxy (4:12, 6:20)? Must Timothy avoid godless chatter (6:20)? Timothy must measure up affirmatively to all these considerations.

Would it be necessary for Paul to inform Timothy that he, Paul, had been appointed a preacher and an apostle, a teacher of the gentiles in faith and truth (2:7)? Would Paul have to assure Timothy, "I speak the truth, I lie not" (2:7)? Is it in character with or necessary for Paul to remind Timothy that he had been a blasphemer, a persecutor, injurious, but since he did these things ignorantly in unbelief he had obtained mercy (1:13-14)? Does Timothy need to be reminded that the household of God is actually the church of the living God, the pillar and ground of truth (3:15)? The whole treatise seems superficial as actual instruction from Paul to Timothy. If Paul at this late stage in the progression of events had to instruct Timothy in this manner we are disposed to wonder what was the nature of his teaching to Timothy when they were together. Such a representation, a letter from Paul to Timothy, is impossible to substantiate from this treatise, and to continue to identify incongruities between Paul and Timothy in I Timothy, even though we have phrased them in the form of questions, is like using battering rams on gates which already stand open, and such a continuation could be likewise absurd and unreasonable.

Is this little treatise actually a letter? It appears that this author is using symbolism, that he is actually instructing the church by appearing to be Paul who is instructing Timothy. If we understand the writer of this treatise as a second century Christian, seeking to give direction on problems in his own day, wishing to gain the authority of Paul to support his instruction at a time when interest in Paul was revived in the church, using "Timothy" as a name which symbolizes the church, this treatise assumes meaning and significance. It appears that Paul has become a special hero for this author, and he is trying to safeguard Christianity in the name of Paul.

The author lifts from Paul's letters Pauline phrases and weaves them into his instructions for the church, but these phrases which he lifts lose their spark and spontaneity and become pointless in their new setting.

122

Does the environment in which I Timothy was produced--Timothy left by Paul in Ephesus (1:3); a church organization with a settled ministry which has replaced the itinerant apostles, prophets and teachers (3:1-13); the absence of parousia; a swing over to piety and good works (2:2, 3:16, 4:7, 8, 5:4, 5:3, 5, 11); ordination by laying on of hands by the presbyter (4:14)--reflected in this letter fit into the environment of Paul's life? Did Paul, when after three and one-half years he left Ephesus, go into Galatia and Macedonia and Achaia and leave Timothy in Ephesus? After Timothy had been such a failure on his mission to Corinth would Paul have left him in charge of the church in Ephesus? Or did he take Timothy with him? Paul sends greetings to the Corinthians from Timothy in Macedonia while in process of taking up the collections from his churches, shortly before his final visit to Corinth, and it appears that Timothy is by his side. Has the church in I Timothy reached the age of the monarchical bishop? It seems so. Does the precaution about enrolled widows (5:9) reveal a stage in the church later than Paul's time? We judge so. Is the mention of fables and endless genealogies (1:4), the ascetic prohibition of marriage and the eating of meat (4:3), the allowance of a little wine for medicinal purposes as a polemic against the asceticism of substituting water for wine in the Lord's supper (5:23), the warning against knowledge which is falsely so called (6:20) reflective of a second century gnostic environment? It seems to be. Did Paul usually draw clear lines of demarcation between himself and his opponents? He did. Is it characteristic for Paul to say, "and if there be any other thing contrary to sound doctrine" (5:19), in reference to something which he might have overlooked? Certainly not. Has the church reached a stage in its development when orthodoxy is forming, in opposition to embryonic heresies? Things are moving in that direction. Are piety and good works replacing the faith of Paul in the church? "Piety" occurs a dozen times plus in I Timothy, II Timothy and Titus (2:2, 3:16, 4:7, 8, 5:4, 6:3, 5, 11, II Timothy 3:5, 12, Titus 1:1, 2:12), but not once in Paul's letters to his churches. Piety is moving to the forefront as a Christian virtue more vital than faith.

Did Paul write I Timothy? We can find nothing to substantiate the Pauline authorship of this letter. This author, except for Paul's ideas which he lifted out of context from Paul's letters, uses a vastly nonPauline vocabulary. He uses ninety-six words which do not appear in Paul's letters to his churches. How many times does "faithful is the saying" occur in I Timothy? Three times (1:15, 3:1, 4:9). Where else does this phrase occur in the New Testament? Only in II Timothy 2:11 and Titus 3:8. This phrase is not typical of Paul. Does this vocabulary reveal anything about the authorship of I Timothy? It only stands in further verification of our judgment that Paul is not the author of this little treatise.

II Timothy.--Does II Timothy, like I Timothy, appear to be a letter written by Paul to Timothy? It appears so to be (1:1-2). And is this letter similar in structure and phraseology to I Timothy? It is, but it goes a bit further and gives insights into traditions about Paul which are not mentioned in I Timothy. How many words occur in II

123

Timothy which are not in Paul's letters to his churches? A total of sixty words. How many times does "faithful is the saying" occur in II Timothy? One time (2:11). Similarities between these two treatises are also to be found with Titus. What do these similarities suggest? Most probably one person wrote all three of these treatises.

Does this little production fit into a real life situation of Paul? It does not, and the reflections in II Timothy assume superficiality when any attempt is made to relate them to actual incidents in the life of Paul.

Does Paul ever relate that he worked in Antioch, Iconium and Lystra (3:11)? The author of The Acts (14:14-23) relates that Paul worked in these cities, but Paul is unaware that he was ever there. Already in the second century traditions dominate the reflections of the church on Paul. Did Paul want to go to Rome? He expresses this wish to the Romans, and he thinks that his visit to them will soon materialize (Rom. 1:11-13). Where is Paul at the writing of II Timothy, or rather where is he represented as being? He is in prison in Rome (1:8, 17, 2:9, 4:16). But did Paul in reality ever get to Rome? The author of The Acts invented such a trip (Acts 27:1-28:16), taking Paul to Rome as a prisoner, so that Paul's fondest dreams could be fulfilled, and the author of II Timothy could well have been influenced by this disposition. But we have no evidence whatever to support the claim that Paul reached Rome either as a prisoner or as a free man.

Is anyone with Paul? Luke is by his side (4:11). What request does Paul make of Timothy? That he shall bring Mark with him as soon as he can come to Rome, that he shall bring Paul's cloak which he left with Carpus in Troas and also Paul's books and parchments, and that he shall come before winter (4:11, 13, 21). If Paul is in prison in Rome how long would his cloak, books and parchments have been in Troas? Paul last visited Troas in late 54 A.D. after collecting in Galatia their gifts for the Jerusalem poor. Several years would have passed. Where is Trophimus? Where did Paul leave him? Paul left Trophimus in Miletus (4:20, see Acts 21:29). How long would Trophimus have been on his sick bed at the time when Paul would have written II Timothy? He would have been there for a long time. This whole situation described in II Timothy has given rise to the speculation that after two years in Rome Paul was set free. He then went to Crete, Macedonia and Ephesus, left Timothy in Ephesus and returned to Rome where he was rearrested and confined in Rome where he wrote the Pastoral Epistles, then died soon after his arrest. Is there any evidence to support this speculation? Absolutely none. Did Paul hope to go to Spain? He did (Rom. 15:28). Did he go to Spain? The author of I Clement (5:6, 7) seems to think so. Romance sometimes takes over where the facts end, and the early church, aware of Paul's desire which he never realized, invented a trip to Spain for Paul so that everything which he hoped to do would be fulfilled.

Do the contents of II Timothy sound like the kind of things which Paul would write to Timothy? Would Paul have to inform Timothy: "For this gospel I was appointed a preacher and apostle and teacher" (1:11)?

124

Is it arrogant, boastful, in bad taste for Paul to write: "I have kept the faith" (4:7)? Is "faith" the important thing in the church, or does it become apparent in II Timothy that the important thing is to adhere to a structure of the church and its morals? Would Timothy after many years with Paul have to be reminded to "follow the pattern of the sound words which you heard from me" (1:13), to "guard the truth which has been entrusted to you" (1:14)? Where did Paul in his letters to his churches refer to Jesus as descended from David? Only once, in Romans 1:3. Does this reference in II Timothy 2:8 come through awkwardly? It appears to. Why would Paul have to keep reminding Timothy to avoid godless chatter (2:16)? Are we to judge that Timothy needed to have this kind of instruction because of his tendency to gossip? Did Paul warn vindictively of false teachers in his other letters? Certainly not in the fashion here demonstrated. In a church where there is no orthodoxy can there by any heretics or false teachers (2:17-18, 4:3)? Certainly not. When was orthodoxy identified? Near the middle of the second century, and later. Does the author of II Timothy regard Timothy as a very young person (2:22)? He seems to, probably as a reflection on Paul's comments about Timothy to the Corinthians. How old would Timothy have been at this late stage in Paul's life? He would have been certainly fairly aged. Does this author delight, possibly derive sadistic satisfaction, in listing the arrogance and misdemeanors of others? He seems to (3:1-4). Does this sound like Paul? Never!

What are the scriptures which Timothy would have known from childhood (3:15)? He would have known The Law and the Prophets. If Paul actually wrote "All scripture is inspired . . ." (3:16) to what scripture would he have been referring? What was scripture in Paul's day? Scripture in Paul's day was The Law and the Prophets. The Hagiagrapha had not yet been added to The Law and the Prophets, so Paul's use of scripture could not have included the completed Old Testament. As the church went into the second century Paul's letters and the Gospels had been collected and by the middle of the second century were read in the assembly along with portions of The Law and the Prophets. By 175 A.D. the church was referring to the New Testament. If Paul actually wrote II Timothy he could not have been referring to the New Testament in "all scripture is inspired" because the New Testament did not yet exist in his day, was unknown to the church and some of it was not yet written. It took the church three centuries to identify what was distinctively Christian scripture; and the eastern and western churches still disagree on The Apocalypse and The Shepherd of Hermas. To use these words to support the inspiration of the New Testament is to misuse them.

The author of II Timothy tends to borrow words and phrases from Paul's letters somewhat moreso than I Timothy and Titus, and as in these other treatises these words and phrases lose their Pauline sting, only to seem awkward and out of place when lifted out of context and put into II Timothy. What do these observations about II Timothy tell us about the authorship of this work? They tell us that Paul is not its author.

125

Titus.--Do we get the idea when reading Titus that it is a letter from Paul to Titus? We cannot avoid this impression (1:1-4). What is the aim and purpose of this little treatise? To instruct Titus along with all men to renounce worldly passions; and to live sober, upright and godly lives in this world (2:12).

Where is Titus supposed to be working? In Crete (1:5). Paul appears to have been there with Titus, and left him there to organize the churches in every town and supervise their growth. Was Paul ever in Crete really with Titus? We have no evidence to support the suggestion that he was, and we cannot accept this letter as representing an actual situation in which Paul is writing to Titus. It seems unreasonable for Paul to regard the Cretans as liars, evil beasts, lazy gluttons (1:12). Paul appears to instruct Titus on the kind of men Titus is to appoint as bishops of the churches (1:6-9), but from Paul's disposition toward the Cretans it would seem impossible to find any who qualify, so that Paul has assigned Titus to a task which by virtue of the nature of the people of Crete is doomed to fail. But most of the treatise is devoted to instructing Titus how to conduct himself (2:1-15, 3:1-11).

Did Paul write this as a letter to Titus? Every consideration rises up to negate its Pauline authorship. It is intimately joined to I Timothy and II Timothy not only by professed authorship but by structure, phraseology, vocabulary and purpose. How many times does "faithful is the saying" occur in Titus. Once (3:8). Where else does this expression occur in the New Testament? Only in the two other Pastoral Epistles. Is this phrase typical of Paul? Certainly not. It never appears in his letters to his churches.

How many words occur in Titus which are not found in Paul's letters to his churches? A total of forty-three, many of which occur also in I Timothy and II Timothy, often as conjunctions, particles and adverbs. The words in Titus for virtues and vices are not the same as those in Paul's letters to his churches. And often when Titus uses words found in Paul's letters to his churches they assume a totally different meaning. Titus does not contain the structure of Paul's letters nor the closely knit arguments of Paul's letters.

Does Titus reflect an age in the church when Paul was active, an age of itinerant apostles, prophets and teachers who are spiritually gifted, or is it an age of a settled ministry? The settled ministry has indeed taken over, which tendency was encouraged throughout the first half of the second century. The monarchical bishop has evolved, the itinerants are encouraged to become settled pastors, and many churches preferred as their bishop previous itinerants who possessed a charisma of the spirit.

Did Paul expect a speedy return of Jesus? He did. Do we find any trace of this in Titus? Not the slightest. Do these promptings for an orderly and settled ministry along with a secure organization reveal that life is expected to continue on earth for some time? It does, and the church has forfeited an expectation of a speedy return of Jesus.

Did Paul emphasize death to the flesh and a new life to the spirit, the new man putting on Messiah? He did. Do we find this disposition in _Titus_? No.

Did Paul stress "faith" as the way a man becomes identified with Messiah? Faith was in the forefront of Paul's teachings. Does _Titus_ stress "faith"? No. What does _Titus_ stress? "Piety", a word which Paul never used in his letters to his churches, and "good works".

Does the author draw out fragments from Paul's letters, then piece them together so that they appear to be written by Paul? He does. But do they lose their spontaneity and Pauline flavor in this new context? They do.

What do all these considerations--the church environment of _Titus_, left by Paul in Crete; a church organization with a settled ministry; the absence of parousia; a swing over to piety and good works; vocabulary and style; lifting out of context sayings of Paul from his letters--reflected in this treatise spell out? They reveal indeed that this letter does not fit into the thought and environment of Paul. Paul could not have written this as a letter to Titus.

PART IV

CONCLUSION

CONCLUSION

The Jerusalem nucleus would have been pleased for Paul to have gone somewhere else, far away. They recognized him as an apostle to the gentiles only after eleven years, expecting that he would team with Barnabas on the gentile stage, only to suffer further disappointment. They did not regard Paul as the champion of apostles.

Within forty years after his martyrdom the church mythicized him. And this myth is at its finest in The Acts of the Apostles. We have called attention to the myth as we have examined Paul's reports about himself, so that we can better understand, at least in degree, what the early Christians made of Paul as opposed to Paul's understanding of himself.

We now turn to summarize Paul briefly.

Paul was descended from Abraham, of the tribe of Benjamin, and he was a Pharisee. He first appears on the scene in Damascus as a persecutor of Christians. The risen Jesus appeared in him, late 29 A.D. and clarified the assignment which God had in mind for him before he was born. This credential qualified him equally with the pillars in the Jerusalem church.

But Paul did not go to Jerusalem immediately to claim his birthright. From Damascus he went preaching the gospel throughout Arabia, returned to Damascus, and after three years, late 32 A.D. or early 33 A.D., he made his first trip to Jerusalem. He visited Peter for fifteen days, during which visit he met James, but remained unknown by sight to the churches in Judea. Peter refused to give him the recognition which he sought, so he turned to the regions of Syria and Cilicia where he worked for eleven years.

Fourteen years after the risen Jesus appeared in him, and after working for eleven years in Syria and Cilicia, late 43 A.D. or early 44 A.D., Barnabas located Paul and invited him to visit the pillars in Jerusalem. As they traveled together to Jerusalem, Paul's second trip to Jerusalem, Barnabas and Paul made tentative plans to work together in the gentile world. The pillars--Peter, James and John--gave them their approval, and requested that they remember the poor. Barnabas and Paul, along with Titus who made the trip with them, returned to Antioch.

Peter then visited Barnabas and Paul in Antioch to help them plan their conquest of the gentile world with the gospel. Emissaries from James soon followed, Peter demonstrated a degree of duplicity, Barnabas supported Peter, Paul rebuked Peter publicly and used the occasion to dissolve his plans to work with Barnabas.

Paul probably turned first to revisit his churches in Syria and Cilicia to report that the Jerusalem nucleus has given him their approval, and to bid them farewell, an errand which would well have carried him into early 45 A.D., then set out for Europe.

He traveled no doubt by boat from Antioch of Syria to Philippi of Macedonia, arriving in Philippi no later than 46 A.D., where he worked for at least two years. He was imprisoned in Philippi.

Paul removed to Thessalonica 48 A.D. for a two year stay, to build his church in Thessalonica.

In 50 A.D. he moved on to Athens, was unable to make any converts among the Athenians, sent Timothy back to Thessalonica in response to a messenger who reported problems in Thessalonica, moved on to Corinth with Silas where Timothy rejoined them carrying to Paul a letter from the Thessalonian Christians. Paul wrote I Thessalonians 50 A.D.

After one and one-half years in Corinth Paul traveled to Ephesus, in mid 51 A.D., where he could supervise his churches from a distance and have the advantage of meeting the numerous itinerant apostles, prophets and teachers who nourished the churches of the Mediterranean world. After several months in Ephesus Paul traveled to Galatia by way of Troas and during the next year, through most of 52 A.D., he established his churches in Galatia.

Paul returned to Ephesus 53 A.D. to learn from an itinerant of problems in Corinth. Paul wrote I Corinthians 53 A.D., maybe 54 A.D., and the Corinthians responded by sending a letter carried by Stephanus, Fortunatus and Achaicus. Meanwhile some servants from the household of Chloe reported to Paul of the Corinthian problems. Paul wrote II Corinthians in response to the letter from Corinth and the reports which he received, and the three Corinthians carried this letter back to Corinth.

During the time which passed between Paul's writing I Corinthians and II Corinthians Paul was imprisoned in Ephesus. From his prison environment he wrote Philippians, Philemon, Colossians and Laodiceans (known now by the title Ephesians), 53 A.D. or early 54 A.D.

Already, before Paul wrote II Corinthians, he sent Timothy to Corinth by way of Philippi to see if he could help solve their problems. Timothy returned with a distressing report. Paul made a visit to Corinth himself, a stormy visit, his second trip to Corinth, to confront the troublemakers. He returned to Ephesus depressed, thinking he too had failed, learned also of problems in Galatia, and wrote two letters, a severe letter to the Corinthians and the other letter to the foolish Galatians. Titus carried III Corinthians to Corinth.

Paul then set out to receive the collections from his churches for the Jerusalem poor. He agreed with Titus, that, after Galatia, he would go to Troas where they will meet so Titus can give him a report on the Corinthian crisis. When Paul reached Troas Titus had not arrived. Paul was too disturbed to respond favorably to a request to preach to the Troas Christians and left for Macedonia, probably for

Philippi, hoping to meet Titus in route to Troas. Paul and Titus met somewhere in Macedonia. Titus reported that the Corinthian Christians have at last respected Paul's instructions, that the crisis is past. Paul wrote IV Corinthians and Titus delivered it. Paul continued his visitation of his churches in Macedonia to receive their collections, then moved on down to Corinth where he remained for a three month visit.

His collections for Jerusalem are now ready. He wrote a letter to Ephesus which Phoebe carried, now found in Romans 1-14, 16, and Paul might have sent this letter, an excellent summary of the gospel as he preached it, to all his churches in Macedonia and western Asia Minor, but without chapters 15 and 16.

He wants to go to Rome to get acquainted there, and preach the gospel to the Roman Christians, then go on to Spain. He had Tertius his secretary make another copy of his letter to Ephesus, to which he added "in Rome" in what is now Romans 1:7, 15 and to which he added 1:13-14, and to which he added chapter 15 but eliminated chapter 16, and sent it to the Roman Christians, expressing his hope to see them. But first he must deliver the gifts to Jerusalem.

After setting out for Jerusalem Paul disappeared from the scene. We do not know what happened to him. He was probably martyred, 55 A.D. He never reached Jerusalem. He never got to Rome and he did not realize his dream of establishing the gospel in Spain.

The discerning student will want to study carefully the following map of Paul's travels as revealed in his letters.

But this does not end the story of Paul. In 70 A.D. the Romans destroyed temple Judaism. This was a crisis to both the Jewish people and the Christians. The Jewish Christians of Jerusalem moved across the Jordan river and reestablished in Pella. Their Jewish kinfolk moved to Jamnia. Jewish Christianity, removed from the immediate environment of its parent, could not continue its polemic effectively. The Pella colony disappeared so completely that not a single trace of them has survived.

But Christianity did not die with the Pella colony. Paul had written Christianity indellibly on the gentile world. He was the first heretic. The heresy of today is the orthodoxy of tomorrow. The western church today is Pauline. It is not Petrine. It is not Barnabean. It is Pauline. Paul was inventive. We can learn from Paul. He devised a theory of two covenants, one for the Jewish people through Moses, a second for Christians through Jesus. And by so doing he gave the gentiles an independent status in Christianity, not subject to Judaism, not subject to Jewish Christianity. He transgressed the sacred tradition of Jerusalem and gave gentile Christianity a structure which made it possible to survive in the gentile world. He fed the Spirit with the best which he had.

133

Paul's Travels according to Paul

Damascus, into Arabia
    and return to Damascus
Damascus to Jerusalem
Jerusalem to Syria and
    Cilicia which includes
    Antioch
Antioch to Jerusalem,
    and return to Antioch
(Revisitation of churches
    in Syria and Cilicia)
Antioch to Philippi
Philippi to Thessalonica
Thessalonica to Athens
Athens to Corinth
Corinth to Ephesus
Ephesus to Galatia and
    return to Ephesus
Ephesus to Corinth and
    return to Ephesus
Revisitation of churches
    to gather collections
    Galatia
    Troas
    Philippi
    Thessalonica
    Corinth
Set out for Jerusalem
    but disappeared

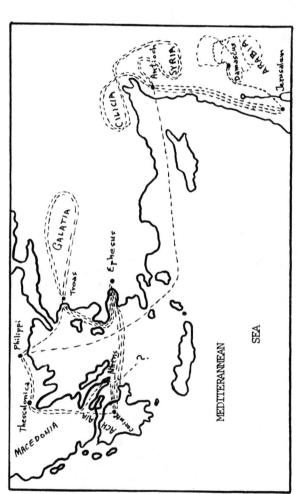

134

What can we learn from Paul and his contemporaries, from the early Christians? We can learn that we too have the freedom to create an authentic form of spirituality for ourselves and for our contemporaries.

In 55 A.D. when Paul left Corinth to deliver the collections to Jerusalem where were all the letters which he had written? They were the property of the various churches to whom he had written them, and we would expect them to be in the custody of the various churches.

One-hundred years later, soon after 150 A.D., what was the status of Paul's letters? A revolution had occurred. Paul's letters had been collected into a compendium. The churches of the Mediterranean world had easy access to them. Portions from them were read, along with sections from The Law and the Prophets, and sections from the gospels, in the Christian assemblies. The church regarded them as sacred literature. By 175 A.D. they were included within that corpus of literature which the church began to refer to as the New Testament.

What is the process by which Paul's letters became canonized? Many of the details are missing. The esteem which Paul achieved in the church and the use which they made of his letters are contributing factors indeed. We are able to reconstruct the process only in part.

When Paul left Corinth did he intend to travel to Jerusalem by boat? It seems that he did. Did anyone in and about Corinth know that Paul and a small band of delegates from his churches were planning to travel to Jerusalem with funds for the Jerusalem Christians? We would tend to think so. Did someone plan to intercept Paul? Was a plot laid against him? The author of The Acts (20:3) relates that Paul learned of a plot against him. Did Paul in his attempt to outwit the intrigue of the plotters suddenly shift his plans and decide to travel by land, and go north probably through Thessalonica and then over to Philippi? The author of The Acts seems to think so. Did Paul write to the Jerusalem church and let them know that he is on his way? We have no reason to think that he did. Did he send a messenger to Thessalonica and to Philippi to report that Paul, even though he had given them his farewell a few months earlier, would soon see them again? We have no reason to judge that he did. Did Paul reach Jerusalem with the collections? We have no evidence that he did. What happened to Paul soon after he left Corinth for Jerusalem? He disappeared from the scene, probably martyred. The Christians in Jerusalem were not expecting him. The Christians in Thessalonica and in Philippi were not expecting him. After the Christians in Rome receive his letter they would be expecting him in the somewhat distant future. How long would it take for the church to become aware that Paul and the small group of delegates from the churches had vanished? One year? Possibly two years?

When Paul was working in Macedonia, Achaia and western Asia Minor, was he regarded as the great apostle of the Mediterranean world? Certainly not. He was in fact relatively unimportant, just one among many. Did martyrdom increase his prestige in the church? It was indeed a guarantee of increased respect and prestige. Did martyrdom lead the churches to treasure their memorabilia of Paul, especially his letters? We think so. What greater treasure could any church have than a letter written to them by their spiritual father!

When did Paul's letters first begin to surface so that he became known to the church as a letter writer? The information which we have begins to come through near the end of the first century.

Clement, who was bishop of Rome 93-97 A.D., instructs the Corinthians, "Take up the epistle of the blessed Paul the apostle" (I Clem. 47:1), then refers to Paul's charge concerning himself and Cephas and Apollos. Clement was aware of Paul's letter which now carries the title I Corinthians. We do not know if he was aware that Paul wrote four letters to Corinth, but we do know that others in the Mediterranean world knew that Paul had written to the Corinthians. Forty years after Paul wrote the church in Corinth still had certainly part of Paul's correspondence, Clement of Rome had access to it, and they held it in high esteem.

Ignatius of Antioch, bishop 110-117 A.D., in his letter to the Ephesians, refers to the apostle's mention of them in every letter (Eph. 12:2). Of Paul's letters Ignatius seems to be acquainted at least superficially with I Thessalonians, II Corinthians (Paul's second letter to Corinth which is now entitled I Corinthians), Philippians, Ephesians, Colossians, Galatians and Romans. Ignatius was best acquainted with II Corinthians (the one which we call I Corinthians). Did Ignatius have access to a collection of Paul's letters? We tend to suspect that he did. Had some sort of collection of Paul's letters been made so that they were available? We think so. Did they at this time bear titles such as "to the Thessalonians", "to the Corinthians", "to the Philippians"? Neither Clement nor Ignatius made use of these titles, so they might not yet have developed. When were these designations added to the letters? To some of them very soon after they were collected. Ignatius in his enthusiasm is somewhat carried away when he states that the apostle Paul mentioned the Ephesians in every letter. Paul mentions the Ephesians only in I Corinthians 15:32, 16:8. Mention of Ephesus sometimes is found in Ephesians 1:1, "who are at Ephesus", but this seems to be a scribal addition rather than from the pen of Paul.

Polycarp, bishop of Smyrna who was martyred 155 A.D., wrote to the Philippians, ". . . Paul . . . when he was absent wrote letters to you . . ." (Phil. 3:2). Did Paul write more than one letter to the Philippians, with which Polycarp was acquainted? Probably not. Is Paul's letter which is addressed to the Philippians as we know it an amalgam of three letters which were separate in Polycarp's day, and which were later joined together? Probably not. Philippians is more probably a single letter which Paul wrote to the Philippians, even though it appears that he finally concluded it on his third attempt, and Polycarp should have used the singular "letter" instead of the plural.

What do these statements of Clement, Ignatius and Polycarp tell us? The churches which Paul established still have the letters which

Paul wrote to them, they are using them, and Paul has become known to the churches of the Mediterranean world as a letter writer because other churches also are using his letters.

Polycarp's letter to the Philippians serves as a cover letter for a collection of Ignatius' letters which Polycarp is sending to the Philippian church in response to a request by the Philippian church (Phil. 13:2). If the letters which Ignatius wrote have been collected and are used by the churches would not the letters which Paul wrote have been collected earlier and made available for the use of the churches? We would judge so. And would collections of Paul's letters have served as an impetus, so as to generate or prompt the desire to collect Ignatius' letters? We think so.

When did collections of letters, collections of any letters, first appear in the early church? During the last generation of the first century. The collection of Paul's letters was probably first. Then appeared the collection of Ignatius' letters. The Apocalypse contains a collection of seven letters addressed to churches in Asia Minor. They were actually intended for all Christians everywhere. What prompted such a collection of letters in an apocalyptic work of this kind? Probably the fact that Paul's letters and Ignatius' letters by this time had been collected and were widely used. Portions from them were no doubt read from time to time in the assemblies. This does not mean that the church considered them canonical. It does not mean that the church considered them inspired. They were simply treasured and read. They were probably first collected by the Christians in Ephesus.

Collecting Paul's letters so the churches could have easier access to them was part of a revived interest in Paul, which moved the author of The Acts to write an account of Paul's activities, how he was stoned, imprisoned, shipwrecked. But this author had no acquaintance with Paul's letters, had never read them, and where tradition was spotty he allows his imagination to fill in the missing parts. He reflects an interest in the martyrdom of Paul, as if Paul was a martyr of sorts throughout his whole life.

What raised Paul's letters to the status of inspired scripture? It resulted from the efforts of a man named Marcion, a teacher from Pontus who was fascinated by Paul and who understood Paul more thoroughly than did any of his contemporaries. He collected Paul's letters, to which he added According to Luke, and insisted that these writings comprise a Christian canon of sacred scripture. Supplementing this action with his teaching, Marcion compelled the church to examine itself as never before. His was the first attempt to form an authoritative Christian canon. He began the process which identified inspired Christian literature. Paul was its first contributor. By the time of Justin Martyr, Paul's letters were read regularly in the Christian assemblies. By 175 A.D. the church distinguished between the Old Testament and the New Testament.

Paul has, after more than a century, become the great apostle to the gentiles, chosen by God to clarify Jesus' message of God's grace, and his letters hold an indisputable place in the inspired canon of Christian literature.

The fact that Marcion who grew up in Pontus was such an intensive scholar on Paul presents us with an occasion for a bit of speculation.

I Peter is a brief document saturated with Pauline thought, and its author used Romans and Laodiceans (Ephesians) freely. And as noteworthy is the fact that he names for the most part the places where Paul worked: Pontus, Galatia, Cappadocia, Asia, and Bithynia. The fact that Marcion understood Paul more thoroughly than anyone else in the Christian world arouses our interest in the reason for the author of I Peter to name Pontus with the places where Paul worked, and in the source of Marcion's understanding of Paul.

Paul worked in Syria and Cilicia for eleven years. Pontus is north on the Black Sea. During his stay in Syria and Cilicia did Paul's travels take him also to Pontus? How much time would he have spent there? Was he personally acquainted with Marcion's father who in time became bishop of the church in Pontus?

The Acts relates that Claudius expelled all Jewish people from Rome. Claudius did not distinguish between Jewish people and Christians. Two of the refugees from Rome, Aquila and Prisca, went to Corinth where they met Paul, and later traveled with Paul to Ephesus. Aquila and Prisca had lived in Pontus before going to Rome. Does the immediate and indestructible cohesion between Paul and this couple from Pontus suggest that this was not their first meeting, that they had known one another from several years back, that they had in fact met in Pontus when Paul visited there? And if so we can easily understand Marcion's interest in Paul, aware of the possibility that Marcion learned of Paul from his father.

But there is more to Paul than this. We want to structure a spirituality which is vital for our time. To succeed in this we need to come to grips with the early generation of Christians. This is no easy task because there is an empty space, a total literary void, no literature produced by the earliest Christians. They did not write literature. When Paul wrote his first letter Christianity was already twenty-two years old. And Christianity was forty-two or more years old when the earliest written gospel appeared.

What can we learn from these early Christians? Surely they contain an echo of the teachings of Jesus. We can learn to feed the hungry, clothe the naked, quench the thirst of the thirsty. We can learn to turn the other cheek, to walk the second mile, to pray for those who abuse us whether psychologically or physically. We can learn how to be born again. And Paul can teach us how to speak in tongues, how to be considerate for the human weaknesses of others in a disposition of forbearance, how to make known the Messiah. Some things about the Christian life are more important than faith. Paul can teach us apage, an intelligent good will toward all. May the apage of Paul overshadow faith, as Paul taught the Corinthians. The arrogance which "the true faith" tends to breed can be overcome only from within. These early Christians can teach us to be human, and when we learn this we will understand that spirituality somehow relates to this kind of humanitarianism.

After we learn these things we are ready to come to grips with our own age. They cannot teach us how to prevent the pollution of air and earth and sea, nor how to tame the atom, nor how to communicate with space travelers from other galaxies. The earliest Christians were fallible, and so are we. They made mistakes, and so do we. But unlike us they were there when it started, and we must go to them to get started again. Since Paul was the earliest to produce Christian literature he is a good place to begin. And if God's nature has any relation at all to understanding things as they are we should not fear to reverse the tendency which mythicized Paul and understand that the most reliable information which we have about him comes from his own pen.

foods sacrificed to idols,
blood, things strangled,
unchastity, 42-44.
foolish Galatians, 55, 132.
forbearance, 104-105, 119-120, 138.
forty lashes minus one, 35-36.
four letters to Corinthian Christians, 108, 136.
"fourteen years ago", 34-35.
Fourth Gospel, 78-79.
fourth letter to Corinthians,
52, 55, 108.
four versions of Romans, 118.
freedom in Galatia, 18, 112-113.

Galatian defection, 55.
Galilee, 33.
Gallio, 81.
Gamaliel, 22, 25.
Gg manuscript, 117.
Gifts from Philippian Christians,
50, 52-53, 67-68, 83, 85.
Gnosticism, 91.
gospel by revelation, 34, 38, 112.
gospels read in assemblies, 120.

Hagiagrapha, 101-102, 125.
Hellenists, 32, 38.
Herod, 28.
"holy apostles", 98.
Homer, 71.
Hymenaeus, 122.

Ignatius, 136-137.
imprisonment in Caesarea, 62-63.
imprisonment in Ephesus, 35-37,
53, 84-85, 87-89.
imprisonment in Philippi, 35-37,
50, 83, 132, 137.
imprisonment in Rome, 63, 86, 124.
imprisonments, 34-35, 50, 53, 62-
63.
incest, 103.
inconsistency between I Thessalonians and II Thessalonians,
75-76.
in route from Jerusalem to
Damascus, 27.
inscription at Delphi, 81.
inspiration of the New Testament,
9-10, 125.
Irenaeus, 118.
Isaiah, 29, 33, 40.

James, 21, 28, 30-34, 37, 39, 42-
44, 111, 113.
James, Peter, John, 30, 35, 40-41,
44, 111, 131.
Jamnia, 133.
Jeremiah, 25, 33, 40.
Jerome, 96.
Jerusalem Council, 37, 42-46.
Jesus appeared in Paul in
Damascus, 22, 28, 33, 35,
111.
Jesus descended from David, 125.
Jesus' return soon and unpre-
dictable, 75.
Jewish Christians move to Pella,
133.
John Mark, 16, 59, 124.
judaizers in Galatia, 112-113.
Justin Martyr, 137.

last days, 72.
letter from Corinthian Christians,
54, 101, 114.
letter from Thessalonian Christians, 20-21, 51, 69-70,
81, 101, 132.
letter to Laodicean Christians,
53, 96-97, 99, 118, 121.
letter to Seneca, 121.
letters canonized, 135.
letters collected, 16, 36, 77,
79, 120, 135-137.
letters from the high priest,
26.
letters incorporated in New
Testament, 135.
letters read in the assemblies
by 150 A.D., 120, 125, 135.
listeners misunderstood, 18.
literary void among early Christians, 22, 138.
lived in Damascus, 26, 28.
loafers, 71-74.
location of Galatia, 55.
Luke, 15-17, 124.

man of lawlessness, 74-75.
Marcion, 96-97, 118, 125, 137-138.
Marcion's canon, 137.
marriage, 103-104.
martyrdom of Paul, 10, 63, 78,
120, 133, 135, 137.
martyrdom of Stephen, 26.

143

145